6316247

DATE DUE
**SUBJECT TO RECALL
AFTER 2 WEEKS**

NORTH DAKOTA STATE UNIVERSITY
LIBRARIES

Local History Collections
in Libraries

Local History Collections
in Libraries

Faye Phillips

Louisiana and Lower Mississippi Valley Collections
Hill Memorial Library
Louisiana State University

LIBRARIES

U N L I M I T E D

A Member of the Greenwood Publishing Group

Westport, Connecticut • London

Libraries Unlimited
A member of Greenwood Publishing Group, Inc.
88 Post Road West,
Westport, CT 06881
www.lu.com

Constance Hardesty, *Project Editor*
Tama J. Serfoss, *Proofreader*
Pamela J. Getchell, *Design and Layout*
Linda Running Bentley, *Indexer*

Library of Congress Cataloging-in-Publication Data

Phillips, Faye.
  Local history collections in libraries / Faye Phillips.
  xi, 164 p. 17x25 cm.
  Includes bibliographical references and index.
  ISBN 1-56308-141-5
  1. Libraries--United States--Special collections--Local history.
I. Title.
Z688.L8P49   1994
026'.973--dc20   94-18399
                                             CIP

P

Contents

List of Figures ix

Acknowledgments xi

1 Introduction 1
The Study of Local History 2
The Nature of Local History Collections 3
   Scope of Materials 3
   Formats of Historical Materials 5
Settings for Local History Collections 7
Notes 9

2 Defining and Building the Local History Collection 10
Collection Development Policies 10
   Defining the Purpose or Mission 12
   Identifying the Patron 13
   Program Priorities and Limitations 14
   Cooperative Agreements 14
   Weeding the Collection 15
Evaluating the Collection 16
   RLG Conspectus 16
   Documentation Strategies 17
Acquisitions 19
   Purchases 19
   Gifts 21
Appraisal of Manuscripts and Archives 28
   Appraisal Criteria 28
   Archival Appraisal 29
   Manuscript Appraisal 32
Professional Organizations 33
Notes 34

3 Maintaining the Local History Collection: Access 37
Print Materials: Cataloging and Classification 38
Archives and Manuscripts: Arrangement and Description 41
Notes 50

4 Maintaining the Local History Collection: Preservation . . . 52
  Security Measures 52
    Segregation of Collection 52
  Environmental Controls 53
  Fire Prevention and Suppression 53
  Shelving and Storage Requirements 56
  Rules for Handling Materials 57
  Housekeeping 63
  Lighting Controls 63
  Insect Damage Controls 63
  Microfilming for Preservation 64
  Document Preservation 66
  Preservation Requirements Survey 70
  The Disaster Plan 71
  Notes 71

5 New Technologies for Access and Preservation 73
  Fiber Optics 73
  American Memory Project 74
  Local and Regional Databases 75
  Commercial Systems 75
  Computer and Fax 77
  Notes 78

6 The Users of Local History Collections 80
  Access 81
    Reference 83
  Copyright 86
  Special Services 88
  Notes 98

7 Public Relations and Outreach 99
  Public Relations 100
    Press Releases 101
    Brochures 103
    Newsletters 103
    Journals 105
  Outreach Programs 106
    Exhibitions 106
    Lectures 110
    Friends Groups and Volunteers 110
    Varied Projects 113
    Review 115
  Notes 117

8 Administration of Local History Collections 119
  Policies and Procedures 119
  Staffing 121
    Performance Evaluations 122
  Planning 124
  Budgeting 126
  Notes 132

Appendix A 133

Appendix B 137

Appendix C 141

Appendix D 147

Bibliography 151

Index 157

List of Figures

Chapter 1 Introduction

Fig. 1.1   Core materials in a local history collection.

Chapter 2 Defining and Building the Local History Collection

Fig. 2.1   Sample list of organizations and people to include in the documentation strategy process.
Fig. 2.2   Deed of gift to Western History Collections.
Fig. 2.3   Sample records retention schedule.
Fig. 2.4   Series that may be found in organizational and business records.

Chapter 3 Maintaining the Local History Collection: Access

Fig. 3.1   Accession record, Western History Collections.
Fig. 3.2   Accession record.
Fig. 3.3   Series and subgroups.
Fig. 3.4   Bibliographic segment of an RLIN record.

Chapter 4 Maintaining the Local History Collection: Preservation

Fig. 4.1   a. LSU Special Collections call slip.
            b. Closed stack material request form.
Fig. 4.2   Preservation supply companies.
Fig. 4.3   a. Request and reference memorandum, Western History Collections.
            b. Patron form, Atlanta History Center.
Fig. 4.4   Regulations for readers, Louisiana and Lower Mississippi Valley Collections.
Fig. 4.5   Basic preservation supplies.
Fig. 4.6   Preliminary processing report.
Fig. 4.7   Preservation log.
Fig. 4.8   Sample field survey form that incorporates condition notes and special handling instructions.

Chapter 6 The Users of Local History Collections

Fig. 6.1   Warning concerning copyright restrictions.
Fig. 6.2   Research aid: Manuscripts.
Fig. 6.3   Photographic reproduction and publication fees.
Fig. 6.4   Photoduplication request form.
Fig. 6.5   Manuscript removal form.

Chapter 7 Public Relations and Outreach

Fig. 7.1   Local history collection public relations plan.
Fig. 7.2   The add-on approach for program development.
Fig. 7.3   Program visitor questionnaire.
Fig. 7.4   Volunteer employment form.
Fig. 7.5   Interviewee release form.

Chapter 8 Administration

Fig. 8.1   Budget definitions.
Fig. 8.2   Federal grant agencies.

Acknowledgments

I would like to thank my colleagues Jane Kenamore, Roy Turnbaugh, and Susan Griggs for their editorial assistance with this project. Robert S. Martin and Jennifer Cargill of the Louisiana State University Libraries have provided support and encouragement. To the staff of the Louisiana and Lower Mississippi Valley Collections of the LSU Libraries, thank you for being there and providing me with the realization that this was a much-needed book. To Patrice Hawkins, a special thank you and my appreciation for your continuous hard work. Finally, I would like to thank my husband, John Bruce, for his assistance, encouragement, support, and patience.

1 Introduction

In *Local History Collections: A Manual for Librarians*, Enid Thompson defined the materials of local history and gave simple advice for handling them. Thompson's manual, a 1978 product of the American Association for State and Local History, is a successful and useful guide for professionals and nonprofessionals involved with the care of local history collections in libraries.[1] Today, the addition of personal computers and national databases to the library world, the development of national standards for arrangement and description of manuscripts and archives, the acknowledgment that collecting policies and documentation strategies are needed,[2] and advances in preservation technology call for a new look at local history collections in libraries.

This comprehensive manual for integrated local history collections deals with administration, acquisition, preservation, access, and use of all forms of materials. It seeks to serve as a guide to the administration, collection, and maintenance of local history collections in libraries. For archivists, the value of this manual is one of continuing practical education and theoretical development as exemplified by the Society of American Archivists Basic Manual Series and Archival Fundamentals Series.[3] The value to librarians is essentially the same, but this book also provides guidelines for administration of nontraditional library materials such as manuscripts. This manual builds upon and is more technical than Thompson's and addresses archivists, manuscripts curators, students, and administrators as well as librarians. It includes information on continually changing areas such as preservation, copyright and other legal concerns, computer applications, and national databases.

Librarians need more technical data than Thompson provides about the arrangement and description of manuscripts and archives. Archivists responsible for cataloging print materials need more detailed technical data. With the advent of personal computers, databases for library applications, and national online databases such as OCLC (Online Computer Library Center), RLIN (Research Libraries Information Network), WLN (Western Library Network), and SOLINET (Southeastern Library Network), not every library needs to do original cataloging on all printed items. Manuscript and archival records can and should be entered into national databases as well.

This manual covers the foregoing topics, plus methodologies for building local history collections. The maintenance and preservation of materials, while making them fully available to the research public, and the basic principles of administration are also discussed. Finally, public relations roles and outreach activities for local history collections are presented.

The Study of Local History

Local history collections focus on local history, and local history focuses on a certain geographic location. Local history has been defined as the study of history from the ground up instead of from the top down. Essentially, it is history from the perspective of a community, state, or region. David J. Russo contends in *Families and Communities: A New View of American History* that the center of power and influence in America shifted first from the local level to the regional level and then to the national level, not from the top down as many history textbook writers have assumed.[4]

The first great wave of interest in the development of regionally focused collections and the writing of professional local history grew from the celebration of the U.S. Centennial in 1876. During the 1960s, many libraries began collecting local and family history materials, and courses on these subjects were added to college curricula. Also in the 1960s, many historians, perhaps as a reaction to changes in society, predicted that an exploration of local history would broaden the concept of national history.[5] The 1976 Bicentennial celebration had an even greater impact. Academic historians now use case studies of individual communities for their research, and history teachers on all levels include regional, state, and local history in their classes. Local history collections, organized properly, facilitate research at all levels.

Today, amateur and professional writers look in depth at the history of minority and ethnic groups in certain geographic locations—small communities, rural and urban, and the social changes within those communities—and at the history of people who left few written records. "Social history involves two broad subject areas that conventional history has largely ignored. First, it deals with ordinary people, rather than the elite. . . . [Also, social history deals with] the history of ordinary activities, institutions, and modes of thought." The great people created less history than we formerly believed, and the unknown have created more. The studies of ordinary people reveal as much about the past and about change as do studies of the elite. This new social history, now more than ever, forces archivists and historians to collect and write local history from the individual up. Social historians hope to create a holistic history that will include all historical aspects: military, political, family, and so on, leaving nothing out and remaking our map of the past. Some authors have achieved this in excellent local studies, but regional and national histories have not yet been written in the same vein.[6]

The Nature of Local History Collections

Scope of Materials

Whether social historians, economic historians, or genealogists, users of local history collections seek information in many types of materials. Printed and published materials focusing on the geographic area covered by the local history collection are important assets. County histories, municipal histories, organizational histories, church histories, and biographies are valuable sources. Local writers' published works, adult and children's work, fiction and nonfiction improve the collection. Local writers may live or have lived in the area or use local settings in their books. City and telephone directories, guidebooks to the area, business directories, organization directories, and local newspapers enhance the collection (see fig. 1.1).

Atlases	Organizational records
Audio recordings	committee files
Biographical dictionaries	correspondence
Books about	financial records
institutions	minutes
people	organizational charts
places	Periodicals and journals
organizations	Personal papers
Broadsides	account books
Brochures	diaries
Census records and indexes	financial records
City, county, and state histories	letters
City directories	memoirs
College catalogs	Photographs
Directories of organizations	Scrapbooks
Ephemera	Telephone books
Institutional records	Video recordings
Maps	Works by local authors
Newspapers	

Fig. 1.1. Core materials in a local history collection.

In addition to books published about the area and books written by citizens of the area, a thorough reference collection is needed. Even if the local history collection is located within a library with a separate reference department, duplicate reference materials housed in the local history collection facilitate research. Atlases, general U.S. histories, *Who's Who*, the *Dictionary of American Biography*, dictionaries in English and foreign languages, and other appropriate reference sources (for example,

The Official Records of the War of the Rebellion) are critical for users of local history collections.

Nonprint materials, such as photographs, slides, drawings, films, and recordings are also important and should address the same subjects covered in the print collection. Nonprint materials, whether computer tapes or glass-plate negatives, supplement the collection's print materials.

Manuscripts and archives acquired by the local history collection will contain print and nonprint items. Manuscripts are "a natural accumulation of documents created or accumulated by an individual or family belonging to him or her and subject to his or her disposition and can also be referred to as personal papers."[7] Archives are the permanently valuable, noncurrent records of organizations, businesses, institutions, and governments. The Society of American Archivists defines archives as (1) the noncurrent records of an organization or institution preserved because of their continuing value; (2) the agency responsible for selecting, preserving, and making available records determined to have permanent or continuing value; (3) the building in which an archival institution is located.[8]

Some local history collections contain both manuscripts and archives. Manuscripts include diaries, account books, journals, logs, scrapbooks, photographs, typescripts, and correspondence to or from individuals. Manuscript groups may be called the papers of an individual or family. Collections of manuscripts are those collected by someone other than the creator. A group titled the "Jack Johnston Collection of Mark Twain" indicates that Johnston collected manuscript material of and about Mark Twain. Johnston did not create the Mark Twain material, but because he brought the items together, the collection bears his name.

Archives may consist of the same types of materials as manuscripts, but they are the records created by an organization, business, institution, or government, as opposed to those created by individuals or families. The archives of a university or business can contain financial records, personnel records, public relations materials, printed materials, correspondence, minutes of meetings, policies and procedure manuals, organizational charts, directories, audiovisual materials, and machine-readable records. The records of other institutions, organizations, and local governments can also contain these items. Sometimes archives and manuscript collections will overlap. A family may give papers that contain business records of the family's lumber mill to the local history collection. Such complications can be made simple by proper finding aids, which will be discussed in chapter 3.

Manuscripts are valuable because they correspond to the information contained in published materials and serve as the basis for primary research. Economics, social life, personal viewpoints, religion, and politics are only a few of the topics found in manuscripts. A diary kept by an early pioneer to the area may dispel or confirm local legends. Letters from a local soldier serving in Vietnam can show the effect war had on the individual, the family, and the community. Photographs taken over several decades depict the growth or decline of an area.

While manuscripts document the lives of individuals, archives document the lives of organizations, institutions, businesses, and governments. Public library local history collections often are designated the official archival repository of the city and county governments. Local history collections in colleges and universities contain the archives of that institution and may also include archival records produced by the League of Women Voters, the Rotary Club, local churches, garden clubs, and fraternities and sororities as well as the business records of banks, florists, lumber mills, and clothing stores. Manuscripts and archival records further the quality and quantity of information about the local area.

Formats of Historical Materials

Archives, manuscripts, print, and nonprint materials have multiple formats such as printed books, family snapshots, computer tapes, measured drawings, and microfilm. Printed materials include books, serials, and pamphlets. Serials are newspapers, magazines, journals, and newsletters printed in or about the local area. Pamphlets can be promotional, descriptive, or general information brochures of local businesses, churches, civic organizations, schools, and governments.

Much printed material, especially newspapers and census records, is available on microfilm. Telephone and city directories currently appear on microfiche. Microfilm and microfiche save storage space, and their durability makes them practical formats. Microform readers and printers are necessary equipment for use of these formats and should be available in the local history collection.

Some maps, such as Sanborn Fire Insurance Company maps, are also available in microform. These maps were produced as early as 1867 as a source for providing proper insurance coverage for buildings in cities across the United States. Shown are the types of buildings, their street locations, and the building materials used. Updated by the company every few years, these maps, compared over time, provide a detailed picture of changes in a city. Whether on microform or paper, maps are a valuable and important source of information for local history. City street maps, survey maps, and topographical maps provide data about the area. Within manuscripts, hand-drawn maps of battle sites, river crossings, and property lines are sometimes found.

Another source of information about buildings in the local area is measured drawings. Architects, engineering firms, building contractors, and interior designers keep records of their work and plans of buildings. A historical file of measured drawings aids in understanding the growth and development and economic and social changes of a community. They are valuable for historical preservation and remodeling of buildings as well.

Audiovisual materials are also important to local history. Photographs, slides, video cassettes, reel-to-reel and cassette tape recordings, phonograph records, and films discuss local people, places, and institutions and how they change. The earliest examples of photography—daguerreotypes and ambrotypes—may be found in personal manuscripts or in the records of photographers. The value of photographs to the local history collection cannot be overstated. They corroborate or disprove both written and verbal sources. Illustrations for publications and promotional materials for businesses can come from the photograph collection. Excellent manuals on collecting and preserving historic photographs are available from the Society of American Archivists and the American Association for State and Local History.[9]

Television news broadcasts, films of college and high school athletic events, professional movies made in the area, promotional films made by the Chamber of Commerce, sound and video recordings of city council hearings, and family videotapes of parades and other local events are invaluable sources of history and culture. For example, the film most often used to show President John F. Kennedy's assassination in Dallas, Texas, was made by a private individual with his home movie camera. Audio formats are also valuable. Recordings of speeches by local personalities, reminiscences of town elders, and music performed by local artists are audio reminders of local history.

One aspect of the audio format is oral history. Oral history is the verbal rendition of folk tales, eyewitness accounts of historical events, or interviews about the life of an individual. Such interviews should be conducted by a professional or volunteer who has done in-depth research on the person to be interviewed and has compiled an appropriate list of questions. Interviews, once transcribed and made available for research, fill gaps in the written record. Oral history is becoming an avenue for completing the historical record of institutions where key decision making is done verbally, such as the U.S. Senate. Through oral history, scholars can gain knowledge about the action of governing boards, city councils, and state legislatures. Another innovation is the videotaping of oral history interviews, thereby creating both an oral and a visual record.

Not all materials for the local history collection are available in their original form. Personal, micro-, and mini-computers are used by writers, school boards, businesses, hospitals, churches, architects, and local governments. Most libraries and archives use computers as well. The original draft of a Pulitzer Prize-winning novel by the most famous of local authors may exist only on computer disk. Because of computers, architects may no longer do preliminary paper sketches of their original ideas for a building. Machine-readable records may be found within manuscript materials. The local writer may donate manuscripts of plays, novels, and poems, printed copies of such items, and the computer disks on which drafts were written, but machine-readable records are difficult for even the most sophisticated and well-financed repositories to manage. Local history collections will be better served if staff encourage donors to print files on paper for preservation.

Archives and manuscripts collections in the local history collection may include three-dimensional objects, for example, swords, dolls, toys, china, silverware, and jewelry. Artifacts more properly belong in the local or state museum, but transfers are not always possible when a local museum does not exist, or the state museum cannot accept more materials. In some instances, if the local history collection is to maintain good donor and community relations, it is best to accept and keep artifacts. Artifacts can be used to enhance displays in the library. When they are kept, they should be identified, cataloged, and made accessible to the collection's researchers.

Artifacts are not the only unusual items found in local history collections. Bumper stickers, political buttons and broadsides, playbills, flyers, art works, underground newspapers and pamphlets, religious manuals, and cookbooks can be valuable to the local history collection. One key to meeting the needs of researchers is to collect all formats and types of materials relating to the local area and integrate them through proper cataloging.

Settings for Local History Collections

Just as local history collections house various types of materials, local history collections are housed in various types of libraries. Universities and colleges, public libraries, special libraries, historical societies, and museums may house local history collections. Universities and colleges traditionally administer local history collections as part of their special collections departments. At Louisiana State University, the Louisiana and Lower Mississippi Valley Collections are an administrative unit of the Special Collections division of the LSU Libraries. The Louisiana and Lower Mississippi Valley Collections contain printed materials by writers of and about the region, Louisiana state documents, Louisiana and Mississippi newspapers, the university archives, and manuscripts covering all subjects in the collections. Local history collections at universities and colleges may be in other departments of the library if special collections are not a separate unit. Some may be an extension of the reference department or part of the public services division.

Though not thought of as local history collections, college and university archives contain a wealth of local history information. While the first purpose of an institutional archive is to preserve the records of the institution, local history is being preserved as well. Records such as minutes of board meetings, public relations activities, alumni organizations, fund-raising ventures, and student affairs document the involvement of citizens in the institution, and its impact on community affairs. The growth—and, conversely, the decline—of the community may be closely tied to the growth or decline of the university.

Public libraries provide extensive local history services to communities. The New York Public Library has collected local history materials since 1910 in the United States History, Local History, and Genealogy Division.

At the United States History, Local History, and Genealogy Division, the collections are a magnet for the American historian. So are the books and records for the genealogist, professional or amateur, tracing down family history. There are also the histories of cities, counties, and towns. For the New Yorker there is precious documentation on the city, ranging from real estate and building brochures to an extensive photographic collection, including old postcards.[10]

As with college and university libraries, local history collections in public libraries often are part of special collections and may or may not be housed in facilities separate from the main library. Smaller public libraries may administer local history as an extension of the reference or public services departments. Such arrangements are necessary when staffs and collections are small.

Local history collections exist in special libraries also. The Newberry Library of Chicago, the Pierpont Morgan Library in New York, and the Huntington Library in California house local history materials. Newberry's Local and Family History Section "has long been recognized as one of the country's leading institutions for the study of local and family history."[11] Private libraries' restrictions on the use of materials may be more strict than those of public, university, and college collections. However, such collections, though not as heavily advertised as those in public institutions, are excellent examples of quality local history collections.

Some local governments administer local history collections in their public libraries. Others choose to place them in state, county, or city archives. Those in state archives often begin as printed reference sources for researchers using archival documents. Photographs, films, and oral history tapes may be collected as an outgrowth of primary reference departments.

Local history collections sometimes develop in hospitals, religious organizations, businesses, civic organizations, and private schools. These serve as a resource for the members of the institutions and staff of the organizations. They seldom are available for public use, although exceptions do occur.

Historical societies have doubled in number since 1976. Serving as community watchdogs for historic preservation gives them an added need for local history materials. Local history collections in historical societies are often part of the library, but in larger societies may comprise a special collections department. Historical society local history collections frequently are available for public use, while duplicate sources may be maintained for staff use only.

Staff research needs are the main reason for local history collections in museums such as living history museums, house museums, and art and cultural museums. Their work of maintaining displays on local history requires reference materials. Often museums will have separate library facilities for these materials and will occasionally make them available for public use if staff limitations permit. Some museums, such as the Buffalo Bill Cody Museum in Cody, Wyoming, maintain local history collections for the use of researchers and visitors to the museum.

Whatever its setting, whether public or private, the local history collection must be administered properly and supported by the parent institution.

Notes

1. Enid T. Thompson, *Local History Collections: A Manual for Librarians* (Nashville, TN: American Association for State and Local History, 1978).

2. Documentation strategies are explained and defined in chapter 2.

3. The Society of American Archivists has published the Basic Manual Series and Archival Fundamentals Series, which include manuals on subjects relating to archives and manuscripts, such as arrangement and description, surveys, appraisal and accessioning, reference and access, security, architectural drawings, reprography, preservation, management, and public programs.

4. David J. Russo, *Families and Communities: A New View of American History* (Nashville, TN: American Association for State and Local History, 1974), 1-2.

5. Page Smith, *As a City upon a Hill: The Town in American History* (New York: Alfred A. Knopf, 1966), vii.

6. Peter N. Stearns, "Introduction: Social History and Its Evolution," in *Expanding the Past: A Reader in Social History, Essays from the Journal of Social History*, ed. by Peter N. Stearns (New York: New York University Press, 1988), 4-5.

7. Maygene Daniels, "Introduction to Archival Terminology," in *A Modern Archives Reader: Basic Readings on Archival Theory and Practice*, ed. Maygene Daniels and Timothy Walch (Washington, DC: National Archives and Records Service, 1984), 341.

8. Lewis J. Bellardo and Lynn Lady Bellardo, *A Glossary for Archivists, Manuscript Curators, and Records Managers* (Chicago: Society of American Archivists, 1991), 3.

9. Mary Lynn Ritzenthaler, Gerald Munoff, and Margery S. Long, *Archives and Manuscripts: Administration of Photographic Collections* (Chicago: Society of American Archivists, 1984); and Robert A. Weinstein and Larry Booth, *Collection, Use, and Care of Historical Photographs* (Nashville, TN: American Association for State and Local History, 1977).

10. Henry Hope Reed, *The New York Public Library: Its Architecture and Decoration* (New York: W. W. Norton, 1986), 163.

11. Peggy Tuck Sinko, *Guide to Local and Family History at the Newberry Library* (Salt Lake City, UT: Ancestry Publishing, 1987), 12.

Defining and Building the Local History Collection

Defining and building the local history collection challenges even the most skillful curator. Determining what has been collected as well as what needs to be collected is an exciting aspect of the curator's job. Documentation strategies, collection development policies, donor relations, planning, policies and procedures, and acquisitions through gifts and purchases are integral parts of building local history collections.

Collection Development Policies

Every library—public, university, college, or private—has its own mission. A state-supported university library seeks to fulfill the larger mission of the university (the library's parent institution) to provide higher education to the public and to serve as a community center of culture and education. The university library seeks, in turn, to collect and make available for students and faculty materials that aid their studies and research. Public libraries, college libraries, and even private libraries seek to collect and make available materials needed by their patrons.

In order to carry out its role in the mission of the parent institution, each local history collection needs a collection development policy. This policy is comparable to a road map that shows where the collection is, where it wants to go, and how best to get there. Specialized departments within the library will have their own collection policies that complement the library's.[1]

Planning begins with a written collection development policy. The American Library Association (ALA) states that a written collection development policy is a tool that assists acquisitions personnel in working consistently toward defined goals, thus ensuring stronger collections with wiser use of resources.[2] A written policy also informs patrons, employees, and administrators of the nature and scope of the collection and of plans for development. Libraries try to identify their patrons' requirements and establish priorities for fulfilling them. A collection development policy addresses the breadth and depth of the collection's focus, whether it is geographic, subject oriented, or chronological. Policy statements are regularly reviewed so that changes in collecting areas can be indicated.

Collection Development in Libraries: A Treatise by Robert D. Stueart and George B. Miller, Jr., describes the early days of book collecting in the United States as an era of laissez-faire, when all gifts were accepted. This produced collections that were uneven in quality and that varied greatly in quantity. In their study of American library growth, Stueart and Miller found that development was limited to individual libraries and that no cooperative programs existed. Today, however, more planning goes into collection development and quality is a recurring theme.[3] Although libraries can grow without a collection development policy, most need policies to plan, develop, and evaluate the collection as budgets and space continue to shrink.

Although not as common as in libraries, written policies are becoming more important for manuscript and archive repositories. The failure of manuscript curators and archivists to create such policies does not negate the need for them. In 1975, Kenneth Duckett referred to the use of manuscript collecting policies as a modern idea "based upon the intellectual concept that a scholar can best study like or related materials together and upon the economic premise that a curator who is a specialist rather than a generalist can best conserve the institution's resources of talent and money."[4]

Operating with a written collecting policy may be a change in the library; however, the librarian or archivist should use the results of change positively by setting the local history collection on a predetermined course of action, not reaction. The complexity and the inherent instability of the environment for all institutions make the management of change complicated.[5] But written planning documents are outlines of the steps to be taken to reach future goals and are today's design for tomorrow's actions. Effective policies are (1) reflective of the objectives and plans of the organization; (2) consistent; (3) flexible, so that they can be changed as new needs arise; (4) distinguished from rules and procedures (policies allow for latitude but rules and procedures remain firm); and (5) written.[6]

Models assist in planning, evolving, and changing for the future by aiding administrators of local history collections in developing written collecting policies. (See appendix A for a sample collection development policy.) A model collection development policy contains the following elements:

I. Statement of purpose of the institution and/or collection

II. Types of programs supported by the collection
   A. Research
   B. Exhibits
   C. Community outreach
   D. Publications
   E. Others (specify)

III. Clientele served by the collection
   A. Scholars and professions
   B. Graduate students

    C. Undergraduates
    D. General public
    E. Other (specify)

IV. Priorities and limitations of the collection
    A. Present identified strengths
    B. Present collecting level
    C. Present identified weaknesses
    D. Desired level of collection to meet program needs
    E. Geographic areas collected
    F. Chronological periods collected
    G. Subject areas collected
    H. Languages other than English collected
    I. Forms of materials collected
    J. Exclusions

V. Cooperative agreements affecting the collecting policy

VI. Resource sharing policy

VII. Deaccessioning policy

VIII. Procedures enforcing the collecting policy

IX. Procedures for reviewing the policy and its implementation

Defining the Purpose or Mission

The purpose of the organization is defined in the statement of purpose or mission and is periodically reviewed and analyzed. The local history collection's statement of purpose must be in agreement with, and flow from, that of the parent institution. A local history collection in a university functions within, and helps fulfill the mission of, the university as a whole. A local history collection in a public library assists in fulfilling the mission of the public library system. Historical societies may include a museum, a historic house, and a library, of which the local history collection is a part; as such, the local history collection seeks to promote the mission of the historical society as a whole.

Curators must define the types of programs supported by the collection. The level of research to be served and how that research applies to the collection requires evaluation. The research level is tied closely to institutional affiliation and initial materials acquired. Users and gift givers (donors) can affect developmental focus as well. Through the collection development policy, librarians and archivists determine whether the collection is to be exhaustive in a certain field or complementary to other resources. How the materials of the integrated local history collection are to be used also affects acquisitions.

Exhibits, for example, represent research use. Curators who plan to make exhibits part of their programs specify this in the collecting policy.

It is also important to explain the physical type of exhibit—exhibit cases, traveling exhibits, freestanding exhibits, and so on. Patrons and donors need to know whether exhibits will be available as an aid to research and as a product of their donations.

Community programs referred to as outreach are significant to local history collection in the same way that exhibits are. They provide publicity, bring visits by researchers and donors, and inform the public about the use of the collection. If outreach programs—slide presentations, lecture series, workshops, tours, classes, and so forth—are parts of planned programs, the users and the donors need to be informed.

Publications can be a program function as well. Archivists and librarians planning publications programs can outline the types of publications included in the policies. Publications also serve as outreach activities. In addition to publishing materials from the library, staff may develop newsletters or bulletins, journals or magazines, or even pictorial publications.

Patrons and donors will want to know when funds are available for special projects such as microfilming or retrospective cataloging. Also, many programs overlap. A lecture series, for example, would be part of an outreach program; exhibits and publications could result from it. Another type of program is acquiring grants from agencies, such as the National Endowment for the Humanities (NEH). Inclusion of these elements in policies serves to inform the public, administration, and staff of activities and programs while providing for flexibility in program planning. It also enables the local history collection librarian or archivist to avoid becoming involved in unplanned activities and the acquisition of unwanted materials.

Identifying the Patron

Collection development policies should also define the clientele served by the local history collection. A definition of terms is a critical part of creating policy. Who are scholars, graduate students, and the general public? Are only professors considered scholars, or are freelance writers and others included? If letters of introduction or identification are needed for access, this must be specified in the policy. Although the classification *graduate student* is self-explanatory, some clarification may be needed concerning credentials. Are there any exclusions affecting who may have access to the collection? Are undergraduates permitted? Do pre-college students need to be accompanied by an adult? A local history collection in a small community college can differ distinctly from one in a large metropolitan public library, and collection development activities will vary accordingly.

Program Priorities and Limitations

Priorities and limitations are discussed in the collection development policy. What are the present strengths? How do these strengths meet the needs of the programs and the clientele served? Specify which fields—history, literature, culture, folklore, and so on—are represented most voluminously or qualitatively in materials. What fields, types of materials, or subject areas are collected to an exhaustive (leaving nothing out) or to a comprehensive (including much) degree? Is the collection's purpose to acquire all materials, manuscripts, books, speeches, and so on about a particular person or a particular school or organization? Or is it to preserve a representative sample of all fields and subjects for a particular time or event, for example, the pre-Civil War history of a town, or only folklore materials relating to the county? What materials or subjects are minimally represented in the collection, and will such items continue to be accepted? When two local history collections are located in the same region of a state, one may concentrate on women's history while the other concentrates on folklore. The desired level of collecting to meet the program needs affects all of the priorities and limitations of the collection.

Once program needs are identified, acquisitions can become more focused. Specify the geographic limit of the local history collection: town, county, state, or region. Is it focused on a specific time period, or does it include materials from all periods? What subjects are covered? The collection may focus only on local genealogical information and not the history of businesses in the area. In which languages other than English are items acquired and why? Are materials in Spanish accepted because there is a significant Spanish-speaking population in the area or because the area was settled by Spanish peoples? What forms or formats will be included—microforms, audiovisual items, printed materials, computer records, manuscripts, others? Exclusions should also be a part of the policy. For example, a local history collection might seek everything about the area except local church records, because there is a religious archive in the next town.

Cooperative Agreements

Overlap will occur in some manner with other collections. A county local history collection will contain materials similar to those in the local history collection of a city or university in the same county. Cooperative agreements can help extend limited acquisitions money by preventing the purchase of duplicate published materials. Cooperative agreements are even more important when collecting manuscripts and archives. Family papers may contain the papers of politicians, academicians, scientists, women, African Americans, or organizations and may cover numerous time periods and places. Three local history collections might agree that only one will accept the papers of a certain novelist, even though the novelist lived in the three towns represented. Cooperation is a constant responsibility of the local history collection and is imperative when the acquisition of archival materials is in question. Colleagues can observe what others have accomplished and borrow workable ideas. It is not necessary to reinvent the wheel each time a new local history collection is begun, because many methodologies and procedures can be adapted to each individual collection. Staff can learn from colleagues through participation at regional and national professional organization meetings. Another type of cooperation is to report acquisitions to the general public through newspaper articles and newsletters and to the state historical society; the state library association; and local historical, library, and genealogical societies. Manuscript collections should also be reported to the National Union Catalog of Manuscript Collections at the Library of Congress. Materials in local history collections may also be included in one of the national online databases such as OCLC, RLIN, WLN, or SOLINET. (These databases and their uses are discussed in chapter 3.)

The policy should include a resource-sharing statement. Resource sharing can be a viable part of a local history collection's program. If institutions develop microfilm programs to share unique resources, such as manuscripts and archives, time and travel for researchers is minimized and a wider public reached. Other resource-sharing projects are duplicating audiovisual items for, or donating duplicate reprinted items to, another collection.

Weeding the Collection

If and when the collection focus changes, some types of materials previously acquired may no longer be appropriate. The decision to weed printed materials or deaccession manuscripts or archives needs to be stated as part of the collection development policy. What materials will be considered for deaccessioning or weeding? Will deaccessioned unique items be offered to other local history collections or returned to donors? Will weeded books be donated to others or used for book auctions or other activities? What is the review procedure for items designated to be weeded or deaccessioned?

Procedures outlined in the collection development policy indicate what the staff will and will not do regarding gifts, purchases, exhibits, special programs, research, photocopying, and liability. Of course, other functions can also be contained in collection procedures. The main purpose of procedures is to give staff, administration, and patrons guidelines for carrying out the collection development policy.

Continuous evaluation is a vital part of the total program operation, for it can detect early any imbalance between objectives and policies. Whether part of a six-month or five-year plan, all policies and procedures must be evaluated by staff, administrators, and even patrons to determine if the mission of the collection is being served.

Evaluating the Collection

RLG Conspectus

The Research Libraries Group (RLG) has designed a conspectus (a survey or synopsis) for gathering data to be used to develop cooperative collecting among RLG libraries. Each cooperating library uses the same criteria to indicate strengths and weaknesses with its collection.[7] The RLG Conspectus has been used by the North American Collections Inventory Project, developed in 1983 by the Association of Research Libraries Office of Management Studies, to create an online inventory of research collections to aid scholars in finding required materials. It is also being used by the Library and Information Resources for the Northwest, established in 1984 to assess depth and quality of collections in the region. This group is seeking to establish a shared database for analyzing the information from the assessment project in order to foster and encourage cooperation and resource sharing among all types and sizes of libraries that include local history collections.[8]

How does the conspectus work, and how can it benefit local history collections? Library of Congress classification systems form the general framework, but a Dewey-based version has been developed, too. Also, materials not classified in the LC or Dewey systems, such as theses, government documents, newspapers, and special collections can be described. A subject-by-subject examination of each collection is performed and numerically rated, thus ranking existing collection level, acquisition commitment, and collection goals. Additional comments may be added to describe strengths, weaknesses, and other characteristics of the cataloged collection that are not brought out by the LC or Dewey classification systems.

Methods used to examine the collection include shelf scanning, list checking, the compilation of statistics and citation-reference studies. Shelf scanning gives immediate and tangible results by revealing broken runs of serials, and other problems. List checking is of specialized and selective lists published in subject areas, such as ALA's *Books for College Libraries*. Examples of statistics usefully gathered for conspectus-based collection assessments are the number of volumes added per year, shelflist counts, use of book and periodicals collections, and analysis of interlibrary loan and circulation patterns.[9] The conspectus codes refer to quantity and types of material; they do not rate the collection as good or bad. They simply assist the library in determining what subjects are adequately covered and which need more coverage. Local use of the conspectus helps staff prepare a collection development policy statement. Knowing which parts of the collection are being used and which are not assists in the proper allocation of space and the targeting of areas that need more collection development. Local history collections, using the philosophy and concepts of the RLG Conspectus to assess their collection, benefit by gaining more in-depth information to use in reviewing collection development policies and acquisitions.

Documentation Strategies

Collection development policies are the foundation upon which the local history collection is built. Documentation strategies are the structural framework. These strategies are used to review the current holdings of the local history collection and develop appropriate, ongoing acquisitions based on subject and geographic designations.

A documentation strategy is defined as:

> a plan formulated to assure the documentation of an ongoing issue, activity, or geographic area. . . . The strategy is ordinarily designed, promoted, and in part implemented by an ongoing mechanism involving records creators, administrators (including archivists), and users. The documentation strategy is carried out through the mutual efforts of many institutions and individuals influencing both the creation of the records and the archival retention of a portion of them. The strategy is refined in response to changing conditions and viewpoints.[10]

Advisory groups who aid in acquisitions work and in creating documentation that might otherwise be neglected are a component of this process. Documentation strategies can be established for an integrated local history collection focusing on manuscripts and archives as well as printed materials.

Documentation strategies for local history collections begin by reviewing collection development policies and determining where materials are found that document the local area. Second, a strategy is drafted that asks what materials are currently in the local history collection, what materials are available, which are not and why, how can materials be made available, what are the uses and benefits of materials for the local area, who is interested in the documentation of the area, what current activities and actions are detrimental to full documentation, what can be done to improve documentation, and who can assist? Documentation can include archival materials, print and nonprint published materials, museum artifacts, and government documents. Third, an implementation group is formed to implement and review the strategy. Fourth, the group continually reports on the status on the documentation strategy and recommends changes as needed.[11]

How might such a documentation strategy for the local history collection in a library be outlined? The local history collection librarian of the public library wishes to develop a documentation strategy for the town in which it is located. A planning team meets to define the documentation area and develop a preliminary analysis. For example, the team might define the documentation area as the history of the town from the time of the first Native Americans to the present, and then it would review the collection development policy and highlight areas that may need revision. The planning team then asks other interested individuals to join it in a preliminary analysis of the documentation needed for the area. (Fig. 2.1, on page 18, gives examples of types of organizations and people who should take part in developing a local history documentation strategy.) The planning strategy group discusses the needed components of documentation for the local history collection and begins to write a documentation strategy statement that will inform all local citizens and interested parties about its work and will draw the appropriate people and organizations into the reporting. Certain questions should be asked regarding the various needs and uses that the local history collection addresses.

Participants in Creating the Documentation Strategy

Individuals

Students	Historic preservationists
Teachers	Museum professionals
Librarians	Small business owners
School administrators	Civic leaders
School boards	Government officials
College faculty	
Historians, amateur and professional	

Organizations

Charitable organizations	Lions Club
Civic organizations	Organizations unique to the local area
Ethnic organizations	
Garden clubs	Patriotic associations
Genealogical societies	Political organizations
Historical societies	Professional associations
Kiwanis	Religious organizations
League of Women Voters	Rotary Club

Fig. 2.1. Sample list of organizations and people to include in the documentation strategy process.

The drafting of documentation strategies is an ongoing process that will evolve over time. A suggested approach might be to divide the documentation strategy into several components by subject. First, the planning committee might write a documentation strategy for the local tribe of Native Americans; second, for local churches; and third, for local artists. (See sample documentation strategy in appendix B.) Such division keeps the project moving, makes it as comprehensive as possible, and involves the most people. It also lessens the workload of any one committee and the staff of the local history collection, which, or course, must continue to operate the collection while handling special projects such as documentation strategies. Applying the documentation strategy requires articulation of the need, cooperation among the appropriate people, and support of the parent institution.

Acquisitions

Acquisition of proper items for the local history collection based on collection evaluation and collection development policies can be accomplished through purchases, gifts, deposits, and bequests.

Purchases

Printed materials are usually acquired through purchases. Local history collections require adequate funds to buy books, serials (newspapers and magazines), microforms, maps, and reference items. These funds often come from the library's general acquisitions budget. Once the budget is established for the year, it is divided among the various departments of the library. The local history collection may be able to acquire some current monographs from the parent library's blanket order or approval plan, so staff should review the approval plan books or order lists to make selections. The acquisitions department staff should receive a list of subjects and authors needed for the local history collection in order to purchase books and serials for it.

Some local history collections and special collections departments have endowment funds. Whether purchasing rare books, out-of-print books, maps, photographs, manuscripts, or newspapers, careful selection follows the collection development policy. Ongoing review can always add new topics to the collection development policy.

A "want list" or desiderata of rare and out-of-print materials should be maintained. Such a list will include noncurrent published items that the curator seeks. Book dealers' catalogs, reviewed immediately upon receipt for out-of-print materials, help staff locate needed monographs. The desiderata may be provided to local book dealers for assistance in gathering rare items. Information about book dealers and how to be placed on their mailing lists can be found in *AB Bookman's Weekly* (P.O. Box AB, Clifton, NJ 07015). This publication includes names and addresses of specialist book dealers, the types of materials they sell, and a list of new catalogs available. Another source for such information is *Sheppard's Book Dealers in North American 1986-87: A Directory of Antiquarian and Secondhand Book Dealers in the USA and Canada*, 111th ed. (London: R. Joseph, 1990).

Purchasing single manuscripts—rare books, pamphlets, newspapers, photographs, maps, and fine press or limited-edition publications—requires the local history collection archivist or librarian to work with dealers. A file of dealers who trade in the subject areas and types of materials needed will be useful, as will being placed on mailing lists for catalogs issued by the dealers and for announcements of special sales. Dealers and auction houses, such as Sotheby's, charge a fee for their catalogs, but many dealers do not. Staff should read the catalogs as they arrive in the mail each day, because competition is keen for many items, and good dealers may sell the items in their catalogs quickly. It is standard practice to request items for purchase over the phone. Dealers will mail the requested books with an invoice, and most will allow the library 30-90 days to pay. Items may occasionally be requested from the dealer on approval. When it is necessary to compare the book with one already in the collection, the dealer should be informed that the book is being sought on approval for a specific number of days. Dealers list their policies in catalogs, and these should be followed. Bids may be placed over the telephone at book auctions if a catalog is issued prior to the sale. If local dealers or auction houses handle the types of materials needed for the local history collection, the archivist or librarian should establish good working relationships with them. The sellers need the collection's business, and the collection needs their help. Dealers also are concerned with good public relations and good business practices. Dealers who give false information in their catalogs or who overprice poor-quality items should not be patronized.

Purchases of out-of-print materials for the local history collection tend to be expensive. Items priced in the thousands of dollars must be planned for and special monies allocated to that purpose. Interest from endowment funds may be used, or special grants from organizations, such as the Friends of the Local History Collection or Friends of the Library, may be sought. No matter how the funds are acquired for purchases, the local history collection librarian, archivist, or curator must maintain professional relationships with dealers and donors and know the current fair market value of manuscripts, archives, and out-of-print materials.

> Purchasing manuscripts involves making an estimate of their fair market value—or having them professionally appraised. The field agent who does not regularly purchase manuscripts from dealers may be totally unprepared to make an offer to a donor without considerable research into auction catalogues and other price sources.[12]

The local history collection staff member responsible for acquisitions must research the value of manuscript materials in the local area and in other parts of the country. Reading professional literature, auction catalogs, and newsletters of other local history collections, archives, and libraries can help the acquisitions librarian or archivist learn the current value of manuscripts materials. It is also helpful to establish a good working relationship with one or two professional appraisers who can be called for assistance in determining appropriate prices. Few local history collections have unlimited budgets for the purchase of expensive manuscripts.

Large university and public libraries, as well as private libraries, may have some funds for the purchase of manuscripts and archives, but even they will attempt to persuade donors to take tax deductions and give, instead of sell, manuscripts to the library.

Gifts

All types of acquisitions may come through donations. Proper records on the acquisition must be kept. Deeds of gift, deeds of deposit, and purchase agreements or contracts must specify what is being given, deposited, or purchased. The name, address, and phone number of the donor; any restrictions affecting the materials; and the heirs, if any, who retain rights to the materials should be specified in legal documents. Active organizations that deposit records may retain all ownership rights to those records. If the organization ceases to function, then legal ownership of the records can be transferred to the local history collection.

Because an extensive part of the acquisitions of a local history collection comprises tact, diplomacy, patience, and knowledge are important qualities for acquisition staff. A computerized list or card file of potential donors with notes on materials they may have that are appropriate for the collection is an excellent method for necessary follow-up.

All materials have a physical and intellectual component. Consequently, legal transfer papers must specify what rights, other than physical, are being transferred to the local history collection. Trudy Peterson, writing about donations, states:

> Who holds the copyright? Here is where the distinction between physical property and intellectual property becomes important. It is entirely possible to transfer the physical property to the archives while reserving the copyright in the material for the donor. It is desirable to write into the deed the transfer of the copyright from the donor to the archives; failing that, the deed should specify who holds the copyright and for how long. Of course, a donor cannot transfer copyright to intellectual property unless the donor has created it or has had it legally transferred to him; consequently, most deeds will convey only copyright as the donor holds in the materials donated.[13]

When the local history collection purchases or is given a book, only the book as physical property belongs to the collection. The copyright is owned by the publishers and/or authors as long as it is under copyright.

Donors have the right to convey copyright to the local history collection for items they have created. Copyright to diaries, memoirs, correspondence written by the donor, and photographs taken by the donor can be given to the collection. The copyright to letters received by the donor and of photographs taken by others cannot be given to the local history collection. Copyright transfer can come only from the creator, unless the title has previously been transferred. Clear title must be held by a donor before items are given or sold. If joint title is held, all owners must agree to the gift or purchase. All legal documents must be signed and dated by all donors and a representative of the local history collection (see figures 2.2, on pages 23-25).

It is acceptable to ask donors to give copyright and literary rights to the library. Then, when requests for reprints of materials, new publications, stage adaptations, or movie scripts are received, the library will gain monetarily from royalties attached to ownership of the copyright, as well as providing added resources for researchers. These generous gifts, managed properly, mean added income for the library.[14]

In the United States, copyright is governed by federal law. As Thompson states:

> Newspaper and magazine articles, handbills, brochures, and other published items, intended for public information and dissemination, formerly were covered by the old copyright law. Unpublished works were covered by common law or state statute. The new copyright law replaces this dual system with a single federal statutory law which protects both works copyrighted after September 19, 1906, and all unpublished works as of January 1, 1978.[15]

Text continues on page 26.

DRAFT

DEED OF GIFT
TO
THE UNIVERSITY OF OKLAHOMA
WESTERN HISTORY COLLECTIONS

I, _____, hereinafter referred to as the Donor, hereby give, donate, and convey to the University of Oklahoma for inclusion in the collections of the Western History Collections and for administration therein by the authorities thereof, the following described property:

In making this gift, it is my purpose and intention to vest in the University of Oklahoma all the incidents of absolute ownership of the above-described property, and any additional papers, materials, or other property that I may send to the Western History Collections from time to time in the future, subject to the following terms and conditions:

1. <u>Title</u>. Title to the above-described property, and any additional papers, materials, or other property that I may send to the Western History Collections from time to time in the future, shall pass to the University of Oklahoma as of the date of receipt of said property by the Western History Collections.

2. <u>Access</u>. (Donor should indicate his selection of one of the optional provisions below. Please check one.)

_____ It is the Donor's wish that the papers, materials, and other property donated to the University of Oklahoma by the terms of this instrument be made available for research and/or public view in the Western History Collections as soon as they have been received, arranged, and catalogued. The materials shall be made available for such purposes in accordance with the regulations and policies of the Western History Collections governing access to its holdings.

Fig. 2.2 continues on page 24.

_____ It is the Donor's wish that the papers, materials, and other property donated to the University of Oklahoma by the terms of this instrument be made available for research and/or public view in the Western History Collections. At the same time, it is the Donor's wish to guard against the possibility of these materials being used to embarrass or otherwise injure any living person. Therefore, in furtherance of these objectives, the following stipulations concerning the use of the donated materials are imposed by the Donor:

(a) Identification of specific materials to which access is to be restricted.

(b) Terms and conditions of restricted access e.g., (1) to whom do restrictions apply; (2) who may waive restrictions; (3) who will remove restrictions; and (4) when may restrictions be removed.

All materials not placed under seal in accordance with the foregoing stipulations shall be made available for research and/or public view in accordance with the regulations and policies of the Western History Collections governing access to its holdings.

3. Copyright. (Donor should indicate his selection of one of the optional provisions below. Please check one.)

_____ The Donor hereby gives, donates, and conveys to the University of Oklahoma all literary, artistic, and intellectual property rights in the unpublished materials that have hereby been given or that may later be given by the terms of this instrument to the Western History Collections, including without limitation the right to reproduce, adapt, publish, perform, or publicly display said materials.

_____ The Donor retains to himself/herself during his/her lifetime all literary, artistic, and intellectual property rights in the unpublished materials that have hereby been given or that may later be given by the terms of this instrument to the Western History Collections, following which these rights will become the sole property of the University of Oklahoma.

_____ The Donor retains to <u>himself/herself</u>, <u>his/her</u> heirs, successors, and assigns, all literary, artistic, and intellectual property rights in the unpublished materials that have hereby been given or that may later be given by the terms of this instrument to the Western History Collections.

4. <u>Disposition</u>. Any portions of the papers, materials, and other property donated to the University of Oklahoma by the terms of this instrument that are not retained by the Western History Collections should be disposed of as follows:

(Donor should indicate selection of one of the options below.)
_____ Returned to Donor
_____ Disposed of by the Western History Collections
_____ Other

Signed: _____   _____
                           Name   Date

_____

_____

_____
                           Address

Acceptance: THE UNIVERSITY OF OKLAHOMA

_____   _____
Curator, Western History Collections   Date

Fig. 2.2. Deed of gift to Western History Collections. Reprinted with permission of the Western History Collections, University of Oklahoma Libraries.

U.S. Code, Title 17 U.S. Copyright Office in the Library of Congress, provides an explanation of the schedule of copyright renewals between 1906 and 1978. Anything copyrighted before 1906 is considered in the public domain, that is, the copyright protection has expired. Works still under copyright are subject to fair use restrictions, which are defined under the new copyright law.[16]

Donors who give books, magazines, photographs, maps, and manuscripts may wish to have an appraisal of their gift for tax purposes. Tax appraisals cannot be done by anyone working for, or affiliated with, the local history collection. They must be done by an independent appraiser and must be paid for by the donor. The Internal Revenue Service considers tax appraisals done by the recipient of the materials a conflict of interest. Names of professional appraisers can be obtained from colleagues and other historical agencies. A copy of the appraisal report is sent to the donor and to the local history collection for its donor files. If the gift consists of a large manuscript group requiring preliminary inventorying, it may strain staff resources, because tax appraisals must be done before tax returns are filed by donors. If possible, each group of manuscripts should be briefly reviewed before being made available to the tax appraiser in order to maintain original order and security, for tax appraisers will need to read and handle most of the manuscripts. If the gift is valued at $5,000 or more, the IRS will often request a detailed inventory of the manuscripts from the donor or appraiser or both. The staff must keep complete records of which gifts are to be appraised during the year. Professional tax appraisers should be treated as researchers, working in the reading room under staff supervision.

In recent years changes in tax laws have affected donation of manuscript materials. The Tax Reform Act of 1976 makes it impossible for creators of manuscripts to claim a tax deduction for the full market value. The IRS allows a deduction only for the cost of the pen, ink, and paper needed to create the materials. How does this affect donations? An author may wish to give all of her correspondence and manuscript copies of her books to the collection, but she may deduct only the cost of creating the materials. If she receives a request from a literary auction house to place her manuscripts in an upcoming auction, the author will be paid the amount for which they were auctioned less the auction house commission. Although the author must pay income tax on the money she receives from the auction house, she may benefit more from the sale of the manuscripts than from the tax deduction she would have received by donating her manuscripts to the local history collection. She may also discover that her manuscripts sell for large sums!

Such tax laws create difficulties for libraries that collect manuscripts. An alternative may be to persuade an author to deposit manuscripts at the local history collection with the actual gift to be made at a later date. Donors may also bequeath materials to the local history collection. These are important considerations, for amendments to the 1976 tax law have been presented in Congress and may be passed in the near future.

Roderick Cave in his very useful book, *Rare Book Librarianship* (London: Clive Bingley, 1976), points out that no gift is free. Dealing with tax appraisals is one cost of gifts. Restrictions requested by donors are another. Donors seldom ask for restrictions on the use of printed materials, but restrictions may be requested and needed for manuscripts and archives. Restrictions may also be requested by organizations and institutions depositing their records. Current financial records and records of ongoing court cases should be maintained by the donor organization, not transferred to the archives. Files of settled lawsuits and minutes of closed board meetings can be transferred to the archives. Files may be closed in compliance with the wishes of the donating organization and the law.

Archivists find themselves faced with requirements of the Federal Privacy Act and other relevant state and local laws. Personal details, such as those included in medical, legal, or congressional case files, should not be released to researchers without permission. Information supplied to obtain a particular benefit (veterans' or social security benefits) or to fulfill a legal requirement (driver's license or marriage license applications) should not be made available to researchers. However, this information may be used for statistical purposes, so long as specific names or identifiable information are not divulged. Laws about defamation and the right to privacy must be observed and access to records restricted accordingly.[17]

Donors of private manuscripts may request other restrictions. Such restrictions must be spelled out in the deed of gift, deposit agreement, or will, but permanent restrictions should not be accepted. Restrictions may apply to time or content of the materials or both as needed. A donor may request that certain correspondence be closed or that all papers be closed until his or her death. Whatever the restrictions, they must be clearly stated in the transfer document so that current and future staff, the donor, and the donor's family understand them. Donors may request that materials in their papers that might be found offensive to living persons be closed for twenty years and request the archivist to identify such materials during processing. Staff must be careful that restrictions are not construed by the donor's heirs to mean that normal archival work on the restricted materials may not be performed.[18]

It is an ethical and practical responsibility to accept donor restrictions. However, the local history collection staff must be cautious about accepting unreasonable restrictions. A donor's desire to approve research requests for the use of donated materials is not acceptable. Limited closure of materials that the owner finds sensitive is an alternative to permanent restrictions. Donors may restrict use of their manuscripts to an authorized biographer for a certain period. When a donor retains copyright of materials, researchers will have to request permission to publish directly from the donor. State clearly in the deed of gift or deposit agreement that all restrictions will eventually be removed.[19]

After making a donation, the donor should receive a completed, typed deed of gift or deposit agreement. This should include the appropriate signature from the administrator of the collection, specific information about restrictions, and any other appropriate information. A space should be provided for the signature of the donor and the date signed. One copy is kept by the donor, and the original should be returned to the local history collection for its accessions files. Accompanying the deed is a formal letter thanking the donor for the contribution. Acquisitions librarians and archivists should work with donors to insure that their needs are met, but that restrictions do not hinder researchers' use of materials or staff work.

Donors must not be neglected after they make their gift. Names of donors and descriptions of their gifts should appear in the collection's annual report. If the collection has a newsletter, all donors can be placed on the mailing list to receive not only the newsletter but invitations to all activities of the collection. Donors who have presented gifts to the collection once may donate again and may influence others to do the same. Finally, donors frequently drop in unannounced to visit or telephone to chat. Such visits and calls must be handled with concern and interest, no matter how busy the staff is. Donors can be given guided tours of the nonpublic areas of the collections, but when they ask to use materials, they must work in the research or reading room under the same rules as nondonors. In most cases, donors will appreciate the care and security the collection provides for their materials.

Appraisal of Manuscripts and Archives

Appraisal of manuscripts and archives is defined as "the process of determining whether documentary materials have sufficient value to warrant acquisition by an archival institution."[20] This is the first step in accepting manuscripts or archives for the local history collection. Complete archival groups will contain information on all functions of the organization or institution over its life. (See appendix D for an appraisal checklist.)

Appraisal Criteria

In the 1950s, at the National Archives in Washington, D.C., modern appraisal became the method of dealing with the enormous volume of records the government created during and after World War II. Not every record of the government could be kept permanently in the National Archives, so appraisal criteria were developed to determine which materials were archival. T. R. Schellenberg wrote:

> The values that are inherent in modern public records are two kinds: primary values for the originating agency itself and secondary values for other agencies and private users. The secondary values of public records can be ascertained most easily if they are considered in relation to two kinds of matters:

(1) the evidence they contain of the organization and functioning of the Government body that produced them, and (2) the information they contain on persons, corporate bodies, things, problems, conditions, and the like with which the Government body dealt.[21]

Schellenberg went on to define these two as evidential and information values.

Archival Appraisal

This approach may also be used to appraise the records of local organizations and institutions. Archives of civic clubs, local businesses, churches, hospitals, schools, historical agencies, libraries, and architectural firms include records that were created to accomplish the purposes of the organization. The local League of Women Voters records will contain correspondence and financial records showing how the organization functions. While current records are generally most important to the organization, archival records are valuable to researchers, and for historical studies. For example, correspondence may contain documentation on the life of a leading citizen whose biography is being written by the county historian. Baptismal records of the local Catholic church are another example. These are essential records of the church but they have long been used by genealogists for their personal research. Essential records are those that are necessary for the ongoing business of an agency, without which the agency could not continue to function effectively.

All organizations and institutions share similar types of records. Archival records collected for local history collections may be those of the League of Women Voters, the Rotary Club, local churches, garden clubs, the historic preservation society, lumber mills, factories, florists, morticians, art guilds, and library clubs. To insure that only records of enduring value from such groups are sent to the local history collection, records schedules must be established. For example, federal tax laws require financial records of profit and nonprofit agencies to be kept for seven years from the date of the tax statement. After that time financial records, such as canceled checks and bank statements, may be disposed of according to records schedules. Tax returns, audit statements, and quarterly financial reports are kept for the archives. Other financial materials, vouchers, and invoices, may be destroyed sooner. Correspondence and committee minutes are usually considered permanent archival records. Records schedules designate archival records as well as nonarchival records which may be destroyed after a certain number of years (see fig. 2.3, on page 30). By using records schedules, permanently valuable records can be transferred to the archives and nonarchival materials can be destroyed at the appropriate times.

Schedule Number	Description of Records	Retention
	Emergency Health Services	
400-01	*Administrative Record File* Pertains to the operation of the Office of Emergency Health Services and includes correspondence related to the function of this office: health bulletins, publications, biennial reports (budget and appropriation), personnel records, travel reports, blank forms, memoranda, and other related materials	Destroy after five years
	Consumer Protection Division	
401-01	*License Card File* Shows establishments licensed by the division	Microfilm and destroy after two years
	City Human Relations	
402-01	*Affirmative Action File* Includes clippings, reports, etc., on city, county, and national affirmative action programs, EEO reports	Permanent
402-01	*Project Discrimination File* Includes complaints against private clubs, welfare, utilities, city, media, housing, police, employment, etc. CONFIDENTIAL	Seven years after resolution of case. Bring forward reoccurring cases as needed

Fig. 2.3. Sample records retention schedule.

Local history collection personnel can work with groups whose records they wish to collect to establish records schedules and a proper records management plan. Many times, however, records are received from organizations that have had no records management program. These records may be voluminous, in complete disarray, and in poor condition. Appraisal is an essential first step before the records are accepted for the local history collection.

To begin the appraisal, staff should locate a large work area near where the records are housed. Boxes are arranged according to their contents if possible. For example, boxes labeled correspondence should be together, as should all boxes labeled financial records, and all boxes labeled committee files. Items from one box should not be mixed with items from another nor removed from folders until all boxes have been examined. Brief notes about the contents of each box should be made as it is examined, and these notes should be kept for the accession file. (Accession files are discussed in chapter 3.)

Original order of the records is critical. Original order is "the archival principle that records should be maintained in the order in which they were placed by the organization, individual, or family that created them."[22] Original order means the order in which the records were filed by the organization; it must not be changed by the local history collection staff. Only if it can be determined that all original order has been lost should any files be removed from the order in which they are found.

Organizational charts and filing rules will assist appraisal. As the boxes are reviewed, specific types of materials should begin to appear similar. These series of materials should then be grouped together chronologically. Series are defined as "a body of file units or documents arranged in accordance with a unified filing system or maintained by the records creator as a unit because of some relationship arising out of their creation, receipt, or use."[23] Series will be all officers' correspondence, financial records, committee files, special project files, and the like. (See fig. 2.4 for examples of series found in organizational and business records.) Original order found in the records determines the series. These can be reviewed with an appraisal checklist.

Correspondence
Committee minutes
Chief executive officer files
Executive board minutes
Special projects files
Convention or yearly meeting files
Financial records
Public relations files
Publications
Personnel records
Policy and procedures manuals
Legal files
Legislative files
Bylaws or charter
Organizational charts
Membership or stockholders records

Fig. 2.4. Series that may be found in organizational and business records.

Appraisal is a look at the entire group of records to determine what will be transferred to the archives and what will be left with the organization for eventual destruction. Notes should be made about each series of materials and the dates covered, materials should be arranged as chronologically as possible, and original file folders should be retained with their contents. File folder labels will be important when arrangement and description of the records is done. Also retain any notes included with the records about the files or their contents.

Items that are nonarchival—duplicate copies of the organization's newsletter, copies of the town newspaper available elsewhere, vouchers and invoices for routine office supplies more than three years old, canceled checks and bank statements more than seven years old, and duplicate reading and clipping files—should be eliminated. The archive does not need to keep 100 copies of the organization's promotional brochure. Two brochures should be kept for the organization's records, one should be kept for the local history collection pamphlet or vertical file, and one should be kept for the collection's exhibitions file. Samples of blank stationary and invoices might also be kept for the exhibitions file because of their decorative letterhead.

After the initial appraisal is made, materials should be reboxed and the boxes labeled according to the series they contain. Use acid-free records center cartons. Each box should be properly marked with the name of the organization and numbered to match appraisal notes. A preliminary box label is useful for such purposes. Also label the boxes to be retained by the organization, with suggested dates of destruction. Prepare a transfer form for signature by a representative of the organization and of the local history collection. The form should contain the name, address, telephone number, and contact person for the organization; a description of the records to be transferred; and the name, address, phone number, and contact person for the local history collection.

If there is not room at the organization's offices for appraisal of the records, transfer them to the local history collection's workrooms. Be sure to provide a transfer form to the organization before moving records. Follow all appraisal steps, and return to the organization items that are not wanted for the collection.

Manuscript Appraisal

Appraisal of individual or family papers—manuscripts—is similar to appraisal of organizational records. Original order should be maintained for manuscripts as well as for organizational records. In some cases, the original order of the papers may be completely lost. Practice, patience, and caution are called for in appraisal of personal and family papers in order to determine which items are of enduring value.

Most people have some type of workable filing system. Staff should obtain from the creator of the papers a description of any filing systems and methods of organization. An appraisal checklist and guidelines can be used for appraisal of individual and family manuscripts and papers. Some items, such as some canceled checks, copies of current newspapers, and duplicate items, may be appraised as not historically valuable. Once the appraisal is complete, return unwanted items to the owners with the stipulation that other unwanted materials may be identified and returned at a later date. Ask if other unwanted items should be returned or discarded after processing.

Personal papers are sometimes offered to the local history collection after the death of the creator. In such cases, the creator's filing system and method of organization may be unclear. Correspondence, financial records, memoirs, diaries, recipe files, military papers, school records, and photographs are series found in personal papers. Personal papers may also contain organizational files, because a person who served on a number of professional organization committees will have these files among their personal papers. Indeed, professional files can be a large part of personal papers. For example, family papers given to the local history collection may contain the files of members who were officers of civic organizations, committee members and chairpeople for church and professional groups, and leaders of children's activities such as Boy Scouts and swim teams. Local history collections will greatly enhance the research materials available by collecting family papers.

Professional Organizations

The following organizations offer services that are helpful in building and maintaining local history collections:

Society of American Archivists
600 S. Federal, Suite 504
Chicago, IL 60605
Phone (312) 922-0140
FAX (312) 342-1452
Publishes *American Archivist* and manuals relating to archival work

Society of Georgia Archivists
P.O. Box 261
Georgia State University
Atlanta, GA 30303
Phone (404) 651-2477
Publishes *Provenance* (formerly *Georgia Archive*)

Midwest Archives Conference
c/o Calumet Regional Archives
3400 Broadway
Gary, IN 46408
Publishes *Archival Issues* (formerly the *Midwestern Archivist*)

American Library Association (ALA)
50 E. Huron Street
Chicago, IL 60611
Phone (312) 944-6780
Publishes *American Libraries* and books and manuals

Affiliates of ALA:
Association of College & Research Libraries (ACRL)
Publishes *College & Research Libraries* and *College & Research Libraries News*
Rare Books and Manuscripts Section of ACRL
Publishes *Rare Books & Manuscripts Librarianship*

American Association for State and Local History
530 Church Street, Suite 600
Nashville, TN 37219
Phone (615) 255-2971
FAX (615) 255-2979
Publishes *History News, History News Dispatch*, and manuals and books relating to local history

National Historical Publications and Records Commission
National Archives and Records Administration
National Archives Building
Room 607
Washington, DC 20408
Phone (202) 501-5610
Publishes *Annotation*

Council on Library Resources, Inc.
1785 Massachusetts Avenue, NW
Washington, DC 20036
Phone (202) 483-7474
Publishes *CLR Recent Developments*

Notes

1. Faye Phillips, "Developing Collecting Policies for Manuscript Collections," *American Archivist* 47 (1984): 30-42.

2. American Library Association, "Guidelines for the Formulation of Collection Development Policies," in *Building Library Collections*, ed. by Wallach John Bonk and Rose Mary Magrill, 5th ed. (Metuchen, NJ: Scarecrow Press, 1979), 363-368. These guidelines were approved by the ALA Board of Directors in August 1976.

3. Robert D. Stueart and George B. Miller, Jr., *Collection Development in Libraries: A Treatise* (Greenwich, CT: JAI Press, 1980), 3.

4. Kenneth Duckett, *Modern Manuscripts* (Nashville, TN: American Association for State and Local History, 1975), 2.

5. Robert A. Cooke, "Managing Change in Organizations," in *Management Principles for Nonprofit Agencies and Organizations*, ed. Gerald Zaltman (New York: American Management Association, 1979), 156-157.

6. Robert D. Stueart and John Taylor Eastlick, *Library Management* (Littleton, CO: Libraries Unlimited, 1981), 32.

7. Larry R. Oberg, "Evaluating the Conspectus Approach for Small Library Collections," *College and Research Libraries* 49 (1988): 188.

8. Ibid., 187.

9. Ibid., 188.

10. Helen Samuels, "Who Controls the Past," *American Archivist* 49 (1986): 114.

11. Larry J. Hackman and Joan Warnow-Blewett, "The Documentation Strategy Process: A Model and a Case Study," *American Archivist* 50 (1987): 12-47.

12. Virginia R. Stewart, "A Primer on Manuscript Field Work," in *A Modern Archives Reader: Basic Readings on Archival Theory and Practice*, ed. by. Maygene F. Daniels and Timothy Walch (Washington, DC: National Archives Trust Fund Boards, 1984), 133.

13. Trudy H. Peterson, "The Gift and the Deed," *American Archivist* 42 (1979): 61, 63. See also Gary Peterson and Trudy H. Peterson, *Archives and the Law* (Chicago: Society of American Archivists, 1985), 1-112.

14. Lawrence Dowler, "Deaccessioning Collections: A New Perspective on a Continuing Controversy," in *Archival Choices: Managing the Historical Record in an Age of Abundance*, ed. by Nancy Peace (Lexington, MA: Lexington Books, 1984), 126-131.

15. Enid T. Thompson, *Local History Collections: A Manual for Librarians* (Nashville, TN: American Association for State and Local History, 1978), 41.

16. Ibid.

17. Sandra Hinchey and Sigrid McCausland, "Access and Reference Services," in *Keeping Archives*, ed. Ann E. Pederson (Sydney, Australia: Australian Society of Archivists, 1987), 191.

18. Peterson, "The Gift and the Deed," 64.

19. Ibid., 64-65.

20. Maygene Daniels, "Introduction to Archival Terminology," in *A Modern Archives Reader: Basic Readings on Archival Theory and Practice*, ed. by Maygene Daniels and Timothy Walch (Washington, DC: National Archives and Records Service, 1984), 339.

21. T. R. Schellenberg, "The Appraisal of Modern Public Records," in *A Modern Archives Reader*, 58.

22. Daniels, "Introduction to Archival Terminology," 341.

23. Ibid., 342.

Maintaining the Local History Collection: Access

Intellectual and physical control are essential to the operation of the local history collection, and acquisition of materials constitutes the first step in their establishment. Development of policies and procedures to maintain, preserve, and make materials available for research is the second step. This chapter seeks to provide an introduction to basic access information regarding archives and manuscripts to local history collection staff members trained as librarians and to provide the same regarding print materials (nonarchival and manuscript items) to local history collection staff persons trained as archivists.

The most effective local history collection houses all materials pertaining to the same subject, such as Louisiana history, together with intellectual access and reference in one department. Essentially, a local history collection is a smaller library within the larger parent library. All of the types of materials found in the whole library will be contained in the local history collection as well. It may contain books (monographs); serials (newspapers, magazines, scholarly journals, newsletters, and so on); manuscripts (letters, diaries, drafts of novels, memoirs, daily journals, lecture notes, and so on); archives (the library's and other organizations' records, including board minutes, committee files, financial records, and so on); pamphlets (probably cataloged according to rules for book cataloging); microfilm and microfiche of newspapers, magazines, telephone books, and manuscripts; audiovisual materials (cassette tapes, reel to reel tapes, videotapes, slides, photographs, and art work); government documents, both state and federal; maps; machine-readable materials (computer tapes and disks); and collection-created files such as vertical files and biographical files.

Everything in the local history collection, regardless of type or format, is more valuable when fully accessible. Integrated control and thorough finding aids create the finishing touches for researchers. For most modern libraries, the card catalog has been replaced by a computer. However, card catalogs are still acceptable to librarians, archivists, and the research public. Whether accessed through a computer or through a card catalog, the following searchable elements are necessary for all materials: name of author or creator, title, date of publication or creation, physical format, size, place of publication or creation, subject entries, and location within the library. Just providing this amount of information about each item within the local history collection will consume most of the available time of catalogers and manuscript and archive processors.

Print Materials: Cataloging and Classification

Print materials and some nonprint materials (music, audio/visual, architectural drawings) are cataloged and classified by Library of Congress procedures following the *Anglo-American Cataloguing Rules, Second Edition* (AACR2).[1] The Library of Congress system for cataloging and classification is used by many libraries to assign call numbers to items and to create the basic information about the publications found in card catalogs and online catalogs. Entries in the card catalog or computer online catalog are by title, name of author, and major subjects found in the text. The Dewey Decimal System preceded the Library of Congress cataloging and classification system and operates in essentially the same way. Libraries can use Library of Congress classification numbers and cataloging information by accessing the Library of Congress catalog through OCLC or on microfiche. For items in the collection not in their catalog, the Library of Congress provides cataloging and classification rules to follow for original cataloging.[2]

Catalogs (either manual or online) remain the traditional finding aid for print materials. Catalogs contain main entries, cross references, and call numbers that identify the location of the item on the shelf and make it possible for the book to be removed and then returned to its proper place. Call number classification schemes are based on numbers and letters that identify the subject area. For example, "PS" in Library of Congress classification denotes fiction, while the Dewey number 929.2 designates family histories or genealogies.

Catalog cards or computer catalog data for many libraries are now provided through OCLC (Online Computer Library Center) or RLIN (Research Libraries Information Network).[3] RLIN and OCLC are bibliographic database networks that allow libraries to share cataloging and classification information. Library members are connected online to OCLC's or RLIN's main computers. Cataloging information input by one library can be shared by member libraries, and their catalogers can determine the call numbers and tracings (subject entries) established by the Library of Congress or one of the other member libraries. For example, member libraries might request the catalog cards for Mark Twain's *Huckleberry Finn* as the entries appear in the online catalog, or they may make modifications in the record for use in their own library. The cataloger also indicates to OCLC or RLIN that their library now owns a copy of the book. Copy holdings information is important for in-house computer systems (OCLC and RLIN will provide computer tapes to libraries to load into their own online computer catalogs), interlibrary loan requests, and statewide catalog systems. OCLC and RLIN provide the catalog cards requested, or the library prints out cards directly from OCLC information online. In libraries that have their own online computer databases, catalogers can enter records into the national database and the local database at one time. For example, records from OCLC can be directly input into a local database through a process known as GTO (Generic Transfer Overlay), in which the cataloger locates a record in OCLC and transfers the record to the local database through an in-house computer connection. Local databases may use computer software supplied by commercial companies such as NOTIS, or they may develop their own.[4]

The expense of membership in OCLC or RLIN is prohibitive for many small libraries, so they must receive their catalog information in other ways. Some state libraries perform the function of providing catalog information to public libraries throughout their states. State libraries provide printed volumes, which the cataloger uses to find proper call numbers for the item being cataloged, or state union catalog cards with classification numbers on them. Cataloging and classification information is also available on computer disks and tapes, CD-ROMs (Compact Disc, Read-Only Memory), laser or optical discs, and microfiche.

Libraries can opt to purchase stand-alone computer systems to use with personal computers containing programs for circulation, reference, acquisitions (billing and payment), and cataloging. Many provide the capability to load all information pertaining to the library's catalog and records onto CD-ROMs, enabling patrons and staff to access holdings. Others use a local area network (LAN) to connect all personal computers in the library to a microcomputer tape system. Some systems produce cards for the card catalog, and others are online, so that card systems are no longer necessary. Before purchasing expensive computer systems and software, local history collection staff should talk to colleagues in similar libraries regarding their choices.[5]

Many local history collections and the libraries that house them are not computerized and obtain their cataloging information from microfiche of the Library of Congress card catalog, which they purchase. The National Union Catalog (NUC) contains all materials cataloged by LC with assigned call numbers. NUC is also available in printed volumes, but is not as up-to-date as the online computer database. The volumes can be found at most university and state libraries, however.

Current publications contain Library of Congress cataloging information and call numbers printed on the back of the title page. This "Library of Congress Cataloging-in-Publication data" contains the LC call number for the book and suggested subject entries. Local history collections may copy this information for their card catalogs.

These are the many ways that libraries can obtain the call numbers for books cataloged by others, but how are call numbers assigned for printed materials for which "original" not "copy" cataloging must be done? Catalogers assigned the duties of original cataloging must provide classification (call numbers) and main and subject entries for printed materials that have not already received classification by someone else. Such work is based on Library of Congress or Dewey classification schemes and AACR2 which instructs catalogers in the intricacies of applying catalog entries. Information regarding such cataloging can be found in LC cataloging manuals and AACR2.

Much local history materials will need "original" or first-time cataloging. It is unlikely that another library will have cataloged a 50th anniversary pamphlet for the local First Baptist church. If the local history collection has acquired a large number of such items, it may be more cost-effective to place pamphlets in an alphabetical file and not do full cataloging on them. A separate unclassified pamphlet file can serve as a preliminary and temporary access step. One option is to establish an alphabetical, local subject system, with pamphlets filed under the tile that appears on the cover with subject cross-references (for example, "First Baptist Church," See "50th Anniversary, First Baptist Church" for the previously described pamphlet, or "Boy Scout Troop 4," See "Fire Safety Rules" for a pamphlet published by the Scout Troop).

Another temporary solution to original cataloging backlogs is to utilize the library's online computer catalog system to assign a "locator record" number to the book or pamphlet and then house the items in locator record number order. This tells the patron where to find the item and gives the local history collection preliminary control. Catalogers do full original cataloging of items as they are prioritized by the local history collection staff. A list of titles and cross-references of items in the cataloging backlog maintained by computer or card file will also assist staff and researchers.

The local history collection may also be the repository for state documents. State documents are housed and located by state government documents number or by Library of Congress or Dewey classification numbers. If the state government or the state library provides government document numbers, they can be used to shelve and retrieve state documents. In some libraries, state documents are given LC classification numbers in order to eliminate the need for segregated shelving. LC-classified government documents can be intershelved with other LC-classified items.

Subject headings for materials in the local history collection require consistency. The *Library of Congress Subject Headings* (LCSH) is the standard authority file for establishing subject headings in library collections. LCSH provides a standardized vocabulary of subjects, places, terms, and occupations to be used to more completely describe the contents of a book, pamphlet, microfilm set, or other item. The Library of Congress provides their subject headings list in printed volumes and on microfiche. Some CD-ROMs also contain Library of Congress subject headings and name authority files. Standardized entries of names, corporations, and proper names of places are found in the *Library of Congress Name Authorities* (LCNA).

Proper and consistent subject headings and name entries provide access to other files in the local history collection as well. Vertical files (so called because they are usually kept in file cabinets) that house near-print materials (typed family histories, reports, term papers, and so on), pamphlets, programs, small posters, flyers, and newspaper clippings need subject headings. Vertical files can be filed alphabetically by LC subject headings. Vertical files consisting of clippings taken from the daily newspaper are very useful for small local history collections in communities with only one newspaper. Using the same resources needed to clip newspapers to index the local newspaper is even more effective. Whatever the item or format of the item, the main objective of all cataloging is to provide researchers access to the materials.

Archives and Manuscripts: Arrangement and Description

Cataloging of archives and manuscripts is the last step in the arrangement and description process. The main purpose of arrangement and description is to make primary research materials accessible to researchers. This process is based upon appraisal as discussed in chapter 2.

Appraised materials are accessioned. Accessioning refers to the physical transfer of the materials to an archival institution, and accession refers to the manuscripts or archival records being transferred. The purpose of accessioning is to enable the local history collection staff to gain immediate physical control over the items. Intellectual control comes through arrangement and description.[6]

Each separate group of personal papers (manuscripts) or organizational records (archives) transferred to the local history collection receives a unique accession number. This number permanently identifies each accession. Varying systems of accessioning exist. One of the most often used is one in which the accession number indicates the receipt date of the material. The first group of manuscripts or archives accessioned in 1993 receives as its accession number 93-0001. Each succeeding accession would receive the next number: 93-0002, 93-0003, 93-0004, . . . 93-1234, and so on. Additions to manuscript and archives groups previously accessioned receive the same number as their parent group, for example, 93-0002-A or 93-0002-1.

In cases where accretions are received several years apart, such a system can be confusing. A more effective system for accessioning is one that involves two numbers: an accession number and a manuscript or archives group number. Each separate title receives a manuscript or archives group number. Then each addition of archival records to the collections receives a separate accession number but retains the same archives group number. So, for example, the archives of the Manborn Girls' School would have an archives group number of #1220. Each addition of archival records received from the Manborn Girls' School would receive a separate accession number (90-0044, 91-0032, 92-0021, and so on). Therefore, all the records of the Manborn Girls' School are controlled by the same archives group number, #1220, and yet all accessioned additions to that group will be identified separately, 90-0044, 91-0032, 92-0021, which will also show how many accretions have been received from the institution and the dates of those accretions.

An accession register is a list of accessions received by number and title. The register may be simply a listing of accessions, accession numbers, donors' names, and type of donation. Another type of accession register is one that has a separate data sheet for each accession. The appraisal archivist's notes are attached to accession sheets with information about the donor, size of the accession, and location of the accession in the local history collection stacks (see figures 3.1 and 3.2).

Accession Record: WESTERN HISTORY COLLECTIONS

Accession Number: Collection Title:

Donor:

Address:

Date:

Volume:

Type: Inclusive Dates:

Description (Series):

Subject Areas:

Condition:

Gift:_____   Loan:_____   Deed:_____   Agreement:_____

Separation:

Location:

Comments:

Fig. 3.1. Accession record, Western History Collections. Reprinted with permission of the Western History Collections, University of Oklahoma Libraries.

Location _____ Mss. # _____ Acc. # _____

Cataloging: NOTIS # _____ RLIN # _____

Collection title _____

Collection dates _____ (bulk) _____

Extent: Format (if applicable):
    No. of items _____   Microfilm   _____
    No. of vols. _____   Photocopies   _____
    Linear ft.   _____   Photographic copies   _____
    Other   _____

Date received _____

Acquisition terms: Comments on nature of acquisition _____
  Gift   _____
  Purchase _____ Price $ _____   _____
  Loan   _____
  Other _____   _____

Source:
  Name _____

  Address _____

Restrictions/Donor conditions _____

_____

Date accessioned _____ Date processed _____

Accession/other title (if different from coll. title) _____

Physical condition of collection _____

_____

Description/Comments:

Fig. 3.2. Accession record. Reprinted with permission of the Louisiana and Lower Mississippi Valley Collections, LSU Libraries, Louisiana State University.

Accession files or donor agency files for each separate group should be maintained. The Manborn Girls' School file will contain correspondence between the donors and the local history collection, deeds of gift or deposit, a copy of all accession register information sheets, worksheets pertaining to the group of materials, any publicity generated about the receipt of the materials, appraisal notes, preliminary inventories, and final inventories of the group. Letters from researchers regarding permission to publish or requests for photocopies, plans for microfilming or publication of the finding aids (inventories and indexes) to the group, and any other materials the librarian or archivist feels are important are also included in accession files. The latter may be filed separately, with cross-references to the accession file.

Accession registers and donors' files may be kept manually in notebooks and on index cards, but the data are hard to manipulate. Personal computers create accession registers using word processing software and databases (PCFile, dBase) that make manipulation of the data easy. Personal computers can print lists of accessions arranged by accession number, group number, donor's name, date of accession, or other pertinent information. Computer tracking aids archivists by maintaining information on special procedures needed for each accession, such as tax appraisal, duplication of photographs for the donors, microfilming of loaned material, and other preservation needs. Computers also help track arrangement and description, processing and conservation statistics, and stack maintenance, which involves locating materials in the stacks and space availability. Use of the computer does not lessen the need for accurate record keeping, however. Computers contain only the information input by the staff of the local history collection, and if the information is not accurate, materials can be lost in the stacks.

The RLIN online national database includes a component which allows for accessioning of manuscripts and archives. The archives control (ARC) allows for input of accession number, date of accession, donor, type of accession (gift or deposit), actions needed regarding the accession (tax appraisal, microfilming, and so forth), and the date on which the actions require completion. Once in the ARC, information is accessible only to the institution that input the data. Some off-the-shelf software packages designed for archives and manuscripts also include accessioning capabilities. MicroMARC-AMC is one such database, designed by the University of Michigan; another is the commercial software Minaret.[7]

Gaining physical control of archives and manuscripts is continued through arrangement. Arrangement is preliminary to description or intellectual control. Archive groups received from agencies will have an arrangement determined by its operations, as discussed in the section on appraisal in chapter 2. Provenance-based arrangement indicates that the archive group or manuscript collection is handled according to what individual or what organization created it, not its function. Archival theory has long stated that archival materials and manuscript collections should be arranged by their provenance and in their original order.[8] Although many manuscript curators are confronted with anonymous collections or individual manuscript items, provenance is seldom lost. Original order, however, may be indiscernible in collections received by the local history collection.

The first step in arranging a collection, whether original order is evident or not, is to research the creator, organization, or agency and the activities of the person or institution. Archivists should verify the dates of the materials, confirm personal identifications, review published items about the person or organization, and begin a biographical or agency history file. Such information will assist in clarifying some unclear series and will be used in describing the collection.

An organizational chart is helpful in reviewing the functions of an organization and determining subgroups and series. An organization may have evolved through several decades and several names before becoming the organization from which the archival records were received. The records (the group) may or may not contain subgroups of the predecessor agency. Within each subgroup, series relating to functions will appear. Most organizations have administrative series, committee series, financial series, and public relations series. Within these series will be subseries of correspondence, minutes, press releases, tax files, case files, and others. Within a manuscript group of personal papers, series may be assigned to subgroups created by the archivist (see fig. 3.3, on page 46). If original order is lost, subgroups and series may be determined by the archivist or librarian by type, activity, or function.[9] "Miscellaneous" series should be avoided, but when all possibility of identifying some items is exhausted, a miscellaneous series may be the last resort. Rearrangement of any record group or manuscript collection is undesirable. When the files have already been artificially rearranged by a file clerk or a previous custodian, rearrangement may be necessary to make the files usable by researchers.

The arrangement of the folders within boxes and the order of boxes on the shelves facilitates description if it is consistent. The rehousing of manuscripts and archives groups into acid-free boxes and folders is critical to the proper preservation of the materials. Staff should follow guidelines provided in chapter 4, "Maintaining the Local History Collection: Preservation," for proper housing of collections. Physical housing and arrangement of groups on the repository shelves is basically an in-house decision. However, physical location should make the servicing of materials as easy and efficient as possible. When space permits, all boxes related to one accession are best shelved together. For the preservation of the materials, oversize and nonpaper materials need separation to appropriate shelving. Whenever an item is removed from its group to be housed elsewhere, a transfer form or separation form indicating what has been removed and where it is housed must replace the item. A procedures manual for appraisal, accessioning, and arrangement and description of archival materials should inform staff of preferred methods, and it should be followed and updated consistently.

Series as described in file cabinet headings	Created subgroups to which series assigned
Middletown Republican Party	Political Activities
Saratoga Republican Party	Political Activities
Republican National Conventions	Political Activities
Middletown Chamber of Commerce	Civic Activities
Middletown Chamber, Executive Committee	Civic Activities Business Activities
Bedford Falls Savings and Loan	Business Activities
First National Bank	Civic Activities
Middletown Rotary	Civic Activities
Middletown Elks	Civic Activities
(14 Middletown Groups—1 file each)	Civic Activities
(8 Saratoga Groups—11 files)	Civic Activities
Businessman's Club	Business Activities
Bankers' Roundtable	Civic Activities
Southside Community Center	Civic Activities
Southside Community Center Board	Civic Activities
Southside Community Center, Chairman	Mary Bailey Peter Bailey Collection
Middletown Museum of Art	Mary Bailey
Diaries—Peter Bailey	Personal
Diaries—Mary Bailey	Personal
Correspondence—Family	Personal
Correspondence	Personal
Scrapbooks	Personal
Saratoga State University	Personal
Elm Street House	Civic Activities
Lake Winamonowoc Property	Personal
United Fund	Business Activities
Financial Statements	(To be divided)
Banking Reading Files	(To be divided)
Speeches and Lectures	
Miscellaneous	

Fig. 3.3. Series and subgroups. From Fredric M. Miller, *Arranging and Describing Archives and Manuscripts* (Chicago: Society of American Archivists, 1990), 73. Reprinted with permission of the Society of American Archivists.

Creating descriptions of manuscripts and archives differs from cataloging print materials. There are no title pages, tables of contents, or indexes to aid in the description, and each group is unique in some way. Some parts of the manuscript or archive group may be similar in type or content to other groups, but all are essentially unique. Papers received from members of Congress contain legislative files on specific bills introduced in Congress. These files may be almost identical to those of another legislator in the same state. However, each legislator will have a different approach to the particular piece of legislation, and, therefore, the file will differ from the same legislative file in a colleague's office. Whatever the material, description of manuscripts and archives serves the same purpose as cataloging and classification of print materials—to make them available for research purposes.

Until recently, description of manuscripts and archives has had limited standardization. The National Archives developed procedures for appraisal, arrangement, and description of government records, which most state and local government archives follow. However, standards for manuscripts had been almost nonexistent until the 1980s. National databases have had a tremendous effect on promoting standards for arrangement and description of manuscripts and furthering standards for archives. Manuscripts and archives are described (cataloged) according to Steven Hensen's, *Archives, Personal Papers and Manuscripts II (APPMII)* (Chicago: Society of American Archivists, 1989). Descriptors of archives and manuscript groups may be found in guides to collections; national databases; national guides to finding aids; and in-house inventories, databases, subject indexes, and accession files.

The library community has long utilized the Machine-Readable Cataloging (MARC) format for printed publications. Since 1983, many archival and manuscript repositories have used the MARC format for Archival and Manuscript Control (now USMARC-AMC). Hensen's manual instructs librarians and archivists in the proper use of USMARC-AMC.[10] Computer field tags are given to each descriptor of a group: main entry, title statement, geographic area, time period, physical description, subjects, and others. OCLC, RLIN, and most automated archival systems utilize the USMARC-AMC format (see fig. 3.4, on page 48).

The final step in description is preparing finding aids to the archives or manuscript group. One finding aid is the inventory. Inventories of archives and manuscript groups will contain the same descriptors as the USMARC-AMC records. Inventories contain a scope and content note, a biographical or historical note, series descriptions, a container listing, and subject headings (see appendix C). Description in the inventory should reflect the arrangement of the manuscript or records group. Each subgroup, series, and file must be briefly described. The inventory concludes with a container list or box and folder listings, which gives shelf location and the box and folder numbers in which series and files are located. When preparing inventories of manuscripts and archives to be entered into a computer database such as RLIN or OCLC, certain information is required.

The database must have the following fields to function properly: main entry, title, physical description, dates, and subject headings. Whether a manual or computerized inventory system is used, it is good policy to always include the required information, which can later be inserted into a computerized system using USMARC-AMC.

Each RLIN Archival and Manuscripts Control (AMC) record may contain some or all of the following Machine-Readable Cataloging (MARC) fields:

Control fields — contain data in coded form concerning the record itself.

1XX fields — contain what libraries call main entries. The main entry can be the name of a person or corporate body responsible for the creation of the collection, series, or item.

2XX fields — contain the title statement. The title can be a collection title, series title, item title, or generic title.

3XX fields — contain the physical description of the material being described. This includes quantity, number and type of items, medium, and arrangement.

5XX fields — contain notes, including biographical or historical narrative; collection, series, or item description; administrative histories; provenance notes; and information on finding aids.

6XX fields — contain subject entries and other added entries. These subjects should come from standardized lists. National lists, such as the *Library of Congress Subject Headings*, or local lists may be used.

7XX fields — contain added entries, which are access points in addition to primary creator, title, or subject.

8XX fields — contain information about the repository.

Fig. 3.4. Bibliographic segment of an RLIN record.

Inventories created for archives and manuscript collections within the local history collection are an important part of the finding aids for the collection. As such, the inventories are made available in the reading room of the local history collection. Most computer catalog systems will not have the capacity to hold complete inventories for each archive or manuscript group. National databases such as OCLC and RLIN do allow for extensive inputting from inventories. None, however, have the capacity to hold box and folder listings (container lists) for all of the archive and manuscript records in the national database. Nor do local computer systems for research libraries such as NOTIS Systems have the capacity for holding online complete inventories of their local history collection archives and manuscripts. Such computer records always refer the researcher back to the complete inventories in the local history collection. For libraries that use personal computers with a localized program that functions as the card catalog, the local history collection staff may wish to investigate the software programs that allow access to archive and manuscript inventories online. Archive and manuscript inventories in printed format, however, must be available in the reading room. Researchers doing extensive research need copies of the complete inventory to take with them. Allowing researchers to photocopy inventories on a self-service photocopy machine may be quicker, cheaper, and easier on staff than printing one from the computer database. Archive and manuscript collections sometimes publish a limited number of copies of their major inventories that researchers may purchase. Chadwyck-Healey is currently producing a microfiche publication of inventories of archive and manuscript collections in the United States.[11]

If the local history collection has no immediate plans to input records into a national database or to use a local database, inventories will need to be prepared, following national standards. When the collection automates, manuscript and archives finding aids are practically ready for computer entry. If the local history collection never computerizes but has inventories for manuscripts and archives that match national standards found in other libraries, research is facilitated. In order to maximize research, all elements contained within archive and manuscript inventories should be consistent and standardized. The processing staff who does arrangement and description of these materials is advised to prepare a model inventory on which all future inventories will be based. A procedures manual also aids manuscripts and archives catalogers. Although *AAPMII* is the recommended standard manual for description and online cataloging of manuscripts and archives, an in-house manual further facilitates accurate description. Procedures from OCLC or RLIN, or any other database being used, should also be included in the in-house manual.

Access to all materials can be provided in a centralized catalog, computerized or manual. Local history collection computerized catalogs make all materials dealing with one particular subject available in the system. For example, if a researcher is looking for information on Robert Penn Warren, a computer search under the subject "Robert Penn Warren" causes all multiple entries to appear. The screen displays all books about Robert Penn Warren and materials in government documents, manuscript and archive collections, vertical files, pamphlets, files, and audiovisual files. If the researcher searches under author for "Warren, Robert Penn," then all items in the library written by Robert Penn Warren appear, whether they are manuscript letters, books, or pamphlets for the U.S. government.

Many local history collections in the past have created segregated card catalogs for printed materials and archives and manuscript collections. As more and more archives and manuscript collections are given subject entries based on the standard entries of the Library of Congress subject headings and *APPMII*, such entries can be integrated into the catalog with printed materials. Authority files are as critical to creating proper subject entries of manuscripts and archives as they are to printed materials. Whether manual or computerized, the catalog exists to give access to all local history collection materials within the library. If the parent library has installed a computer system, the local history collection's materials appear in computers located throughout the entire library, not just within those in the local history collection. Some researchers may be unaware of the existence of the local history collection and will find it only because all materials are listed on the library's computer catalog.

Reporting all manuscripts received, arranged, and described by local history collections to the National Union Catalog of Manuscript Collections (NUCMC) at the Library of Congress provides valuable information to researchers throughout the country. In 1989, NUCMC began inputting all records it received from libraries across the country into the RLIN national database. Therefore, local history collections that do not intend to join national databases may have their manuscripts listed in the RLIN database at no cost. NUCMC simply requires that information be reported on the proper forms.

Specialized indexes and bibliographies prepared by the local history collection staff provide added access to the collection. For vertical files, pamphlets files, photograph files, and other files arranged by original subject headings, an index is critical for the researcher to locate required information. Cross-references make the index more useful. Indexes may also be prepared for newspapers, journals, newsletters, and older books that were published without indexes. Such projects are usually beyond the time limitations of collection staff but are excellent projects for volunteers. Subject bibliographies assist researchers as well. Subject bibliographies may include books, pamphlets, magazine articles, unpublished materials, audiovisual materials, and items available in the library outside the local history collection.

Proper access to local history collection materials facilitates the work of researchers. All cataloging, arranging and describing benefits the users of local history collections.

Notes

1. *Anglo-American Cataloguing Rules, Second Edition, 1988 Revision* (Chicago: American Library Association, 1988).

2. Write the Library of Congress Cataloging Division for information on cataloging manuals.

3. OCLC, Online Computer Library Center, Inc., 6565 Frantz Road, Dublin, OH 43017; RLIN, Research Libraries Information Network, Research Libraries Group, Inc., 1200 Villa Street, Mountain View, CA 94041

4. NOTIS is a company that markets and produces software for library functions.

5. Bruce L. Flanders, "Barbarians at the Gate," *American Libraries* 22 (July/August 1991): 668-669. Some companies who market library software packages are: Dynix, 151 East 1700 South, Provo, UT 84606, (801) 375-2770, FAX (801) 373-1889; CLSI, Inc., 320 Nevada Street, Newtonville, MA 02160, 1-800-945-MARC; Gaylord, 1-800-962-9580; and Geac, (214) 490-3482, FAX (214) 960-9728.

6. Maygene Daniels, "Introduction to Archival Terminology," in *A Modern Archives Reader: Basic Readings on Archival Theory and Practice*, ed. by Maygene Daniels and Timothy Walch (Washington, DC: National Archives and Records Service, 1984), 339.

7. Lawrence A. Landis, "Cataloguing Software and the University Archives: MicroMARC-AMC at Oregon State University," and Donald Firsching, "Information Sharing Through Standardization: Minaret at the National Archives of the Episcopal Church," *The Southwestern Archivist* 16 (Fall 1991): 6-8, 32-34. Gencat, Relational Cataloging Software, 1-800-663-8172; FAX (604) 980-9537.

8. For a historical analysis, a discussion of current archival theory, and an in-depth discussion of groups, subgroups, series, and subseries see Fredric M. Miller, *Arranging and Describing Archives and Manuscripts* (Chicago: Society of American Archivists, 1990).

9. See *Art and Architecture Thesaurus* (New York: Oxford University Press, 1990); David B. Gracy II, *Archives and Manuscripts: Arrangement and Description* (Chicago: Society of American Archivists, 1977) [Although Gracy's manual is now out-of-print, it is still an excellent training manual for arrangement and description.]; Helena Zinkham, Patricia D. Cloud, and Hope Mayo, "Providing Access by Form of Material, Genre, and Physical Characteristics: Benefits and Techniques," *American Archivist* 52 (1989): 300-319.

10. For a complete discussion of description of manuscripts and archives see Miller, *Arranging and Describing*, 79-123.

11. Chadwyck-Healey, Inc., 1101 King Street, Alexandria, VA 22314.

Maintaining the Local History Collection: Preservation

Local history collections struggle to maintain a balance between the preservation and use of materials. Providing access to the materials through catalogs, inventories, indexes, and bibliographies is only the first step in caring for them. Proper housing and handling by staff and users and application of accepted preservation methods are critical to the collection's health.

Security Measures

The local history collection is a historical preservation unit of the library that needs stronger than average security measures. Patrons and donors accept reasonable security measures if they are educated about the reasons for higher security. Creating a brochure that explains the purpose of the local history collection and its need for security is an effective way to handle questions.

Segregation of Collection

The most important security requirement of a local history collection is that its stacks be segregated from the library's other stacks. These segregated stacks must be security controlled, with entry limited to local history collection staff. No one should be admitted to the area when the collection is closed. Even if the reading room is combined with the central reading room of the library, it is critical that separate tables be allocated for the use of local history collection materials.

Although many libraries prefer to permit checkout of all nonrare printed materials, it is best not to allow local history collection items to circulate. Circulation causes substantial physical wear and tear and increases the chances that an item could be lost. If possible, the library should acquire a second copy of printed materials for the main, circulating collection of the library. If local history collection printed materials must circulate, a limited circulation period is advisable. Those using local history collection materials, whether at segregated tables in the main reading room or in the local history collection's reading room, should receive only a limited number of items at one time. Such procedures help to deter thefts, which many special collections have experienced in recent years. Upon receiving the materials from a researcher, staff should cross-check a call slip to confirm that the researcher has returned the item.

The use of "call slips" is an excellent security procedure that facilitates accurate record keeping for closed stacks. These slips indicate to whom an item is checked out, what the item is, the date pulled from the shelf, and the name of the staff member retrieving the item. When the researcher returns the item, staff mark the item returned on the call slip, and in some cases, give the researcher a copy. The staff member who reshelves the items initials the call slip (see fig. 4.1a and 4.1b, on pages 54 and 55).

Other security measures for local history collections include registering researchers; providing identification badges for staff, researchers, and visitors; limiting the number of staff keys to closed stacks and security vaults; establishing a small area of high security within the closed stacks for extremely rare materials; and properly training staff in maintaining security procedures.

Environmental Controls

Temperature and humidity control of the stacks, work areas, and reading room is an important part of preservation of unique local history materials. While an ideal temperature for people is 70 degrees, the ideal temperature for paper is 60 to 65 degrees. Items such as photographs, tapes, book bindings, and other materials may require a lower temperature. People are most comfortable at 50 percent humidity, and this is also the best humidity level for most paper materials. Fluctuating temperatures and low humidity cause paper to become brittle and crumble. Swings in temperature and humidity create an environment in which molds and insects can flourish and in which paper and other materials deteriorate. Collection areas must have temperature control 24 hours a day, seven days a week. If the library turns off air conditioning and heating equipment when the building is closed, administrators need to insist on a separate climate control unit for the local history collection stacks. If the climate control can be made available for only the local history collection stacks, the staff must return all materials to the stacks daily.

Fire Prevention and Suppression

Stack areas also need fire and light control. A fire prevention system is vitally important to the local history collection and the entire library. However, sprinkler systems may do more damage than fire, so they must be placed with caution. If a small fire occurs in one area, the sprinkler

Text continues on page 56.

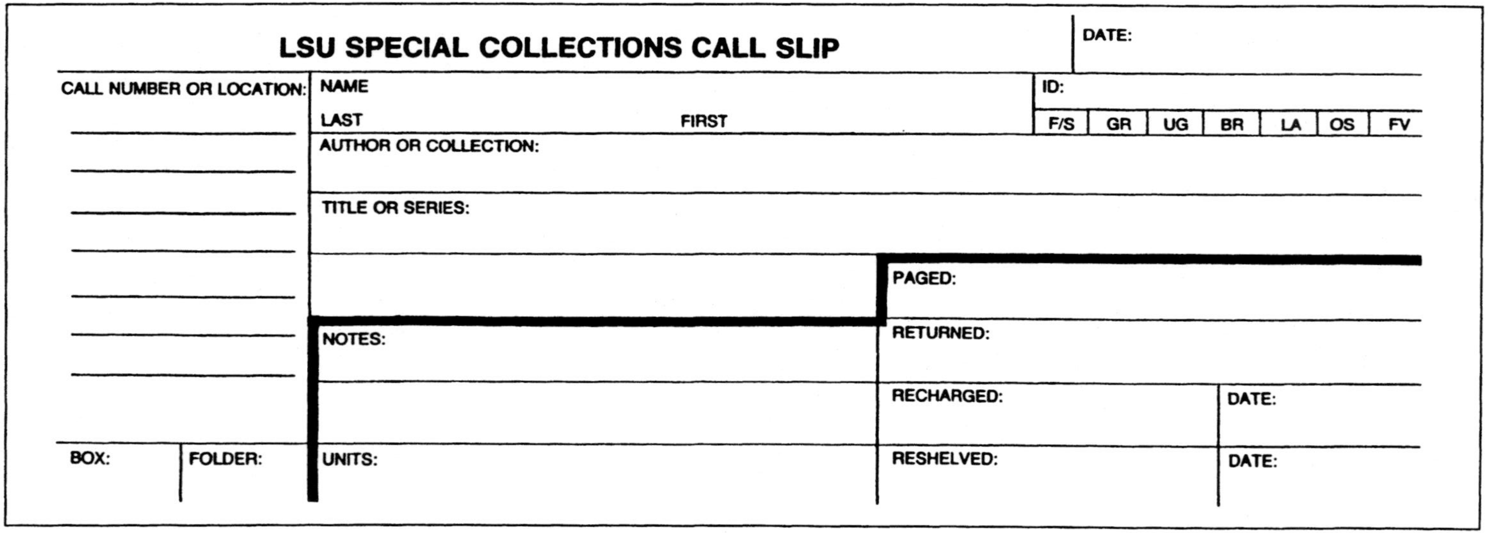

LSU SPECIAL COLLECTIONS CALL SLIP

DATE:

CALL NUMBER OR LOCATION:

NAME

ID:

LAST FIRST

F/S | GR | UG | BR | LA | OS | FV

AUTHOR OR COLLECTION:

TITLE OR SERIES:

PAGED:

NOTES:

RETURNED:

RECHARGED:

DATE:

BOX:

FOLDER:

UNITS:

RESHELVED:

DATE:

Fig. 4.1a. LSU Special Collections call slip. Reprinted with permission of the Louisiana and Lower Mississippi Valley Collections, LSU Libraries, Louisiana State University.

Closed Stack Material Request Form   Atlanta History Center Library/Archives

Please list the items you wish to see. You will be allowed to have one box at a time. Thank you for your cooperation.

Manuscript or Photo #	Box #	Folder #	Staff Use Only

Name:

Please return this form to reference desk.

Fig. 4.1b. Closed stack material request form. Reprinted with permission of the Atlanta Historical Society, Atlanta, Georgia.

system should not activate in other areas until heat or smoke is sensed. Halon, a gas that removes oxygen from the air and thus prevents the spread of fire, has been used in recent years in a number of special collections buildings. Currently, halon is being studied by the Environmental Protection Agency because of concern that it may contribute to the deterioration of the earth's ozone layer. Fire department professionals and colleagues who have assisted in planning fire systems for special collections can aid in developing proper plans for emergencies.[1]

Shelving and Storage Requirements

Storage containers and shelving also require proper planning. Regular library metal shelving is excellent for books, but wider shelving will be needed for manuscripts and archives boxes. Electrical currents can erase tapes; therefore, audio and video cassettes must not be stored on shelves where there is the possibility of electrical currents. Manuscripts and archives, pamphlets, photographs, negatives, glass plates, newspapers, microfilm, ephemera, and all other nonbook or serial publications in the local history collection are best housed in acid-free, lignin-free archival storage containers. Books in the collection that have dust jackets receive added protection from mylar jackets and from not using "seal-in" tapes or other identification tapes requiring glues. Local history collection books need security marking inside their pages. Label only with "identi-strips," bookmarks of acid-free paper on which call number are typed or written. Before purchasing "archival" supplies, local history collection librarians and archivists should consult conservation and preservation manuals and talk to experienced colleagues (see fig. 4.2). The National Archives and Records Administration evaluates various products, and their findings are available upon request.[2]

Conservation Resources
  International, Inc.
8000-H Forbes Place
Springfield, VA 22151
Phone: (703) 321-7730 or
(800) 634-6932
FAX: (703) 321-0629

Light Impressions Corporation
P.O. Box 940
439 Monroe Avenue
Rochester, NY 14603-0940
Phone: (800) 828-6216
FAX: (716) 442-7318

Demco Library Supplies
Archival Products Division
P.O. Box 1488
Madison, WI 53701

BookLab, Inc.
8403 Cross Park Drive
Suite 2-E
Austin, TX 78754
Phone: (512) 837-0479
FAX: (512) 837-9794

Bridgeport National Bindery, Inc.
P.O. Box 289
Agawam, MA 01001
Phone: (800) 223-5083

Fig. 4.2. Preservation supply companies.

Rules for Handling Materials

Once the materials in the local history collection are properly stored and housed, care must be given to their handling. There are less stressful ways to handle books than most patrons and staff members know. Books must never be pulled from the shelf by their caps—the top of the book where fingers seem to fit so conveniently. All libraries have books broken at the top because of this bad habit. To remove a book from the shelf properly, the books to each side of the one required should be pushed back a fraction of an inch and the book grasped by the middle. This reduces handling stress. Pages should never be marked or turned down, nor should the book be lain open face down. Eating and smoking should not be allowed near books; only pencils should be used while handling books. Books should never be stored or transferred in bins. Researchers and staff should place books on foam book cushions when using them. These cushions come in varying sizes and are used to prevent the spines of books from being broken.

Rules for using manuscripts and archival materials are even more stringent. Written rules for use should be distributed when patrons register, and the registration form should require the patron to sign that they have read the rules and agree to observe them (see fig. 4.3a, on pages 58-59, and 4.3b, on pages 60-61). Each local history collection can establish security measures that are appropriate for its library.

Patrons should be encouraged to handle the materials carefully and should be made aware of the importance of the order of the papers within the box. Archivists know that the order is important; patrons probably assume the order is important but need to be encouraged to respect it. Folder numbers on the folders in each collection help patrons and staff keep materials in order. Some archivists stamp folders with "Please keep documents in order." Ink pens, felt markers, and other permanent writing instruments must not be allowed in the reading room. Neither staff nor patrons should use them. Boxes and folders need proper labels telling readers and staff exactly what is being requested and used (see fig 4.4, on page 62).

Photographs, slides, books with rare bindings, drawings, rare maps, pre-twentieth century books containing colored plates, and manuscripts that are extremely fragile or with drawings on them require the use of cotton gloves by patrons and staff. The oil in human hands negatively affects these items, and the less they are touched the longer they will last. Lightweight gloves do not greatly encumber one's ability to handle materials or to write. Any rules applied to patrons must also apply to staff. Patrons will be far more cooperative about wearing gloves if they see the staff also using them.

Text continues on page 63.

REQUEST AND REFERENCE MEMORANDUM—THE WESTERN HISTORY COLLECTIONS

OU-1211-C (Information Provided for Departmental Use only)

Date

Name (last, first):

Address:

Identification: □ Faculty □ Staff □ Administration
□ Graduate Student □ Undergraduate Student
□ Other (please specify):

Telephone:
Area Code (   )

OU or Other
ID Number:

Ext

Institutional/Organizational
Affiliation (if applicable):

Research Topic
and/or
Working Title

Purpose of Research: □ Book □ Article □ M.A. Thesis □ Ph.D. Dissertation
□ Exhibit □ OU Administration/Departmental
□ Class Assignment □ Audio/Visual Item □ Other

Agreement: I have read and agree to abide by the Western History Collections' Reading Room Rules. I agree to indemnify and hold harmless the University, its officers, employees and agents from any and all claims resulting from the use of materials in the Western History Collections.

Signature: _____ Date: _____

May we refer your name to others interested in the same topic? □ Yes □ No

LIST

SPECIFIC

MATERIAL

NEEDED

THIS SECTION WILL BE FILLED OUT BY THE STAFF ATTENDANT

Type of Request: □ Interview □ Letter □ Telephone □ Inter-library Loan □ Referral from: _____ □ Other: _____

Type of Material Supplied: □ Information Only □ Manuscripts □ OU Records □ Publications □ Sound Recordings □ Microforms □ Photographs □ Newspapers
□ Maps □ Other (please specify):

Use of Materials Approved by: _____   Date: _____

Description of Material(s) Supplied/Copied:

Collection Name and Number	Box Number	Folder Number	Copies	Title of Book	Call Number	Copies

Time Required to Answer Request: Hours   Minutes

Attendant(s) Name(s):

Division/Section:

Materials Received by:

Fig. 4.3a. Request and reference memorandum, Western History Collections. Reprinted with permission of the Western History Collections, University of Oklahoma Libraries.

ATLANTA HISTORY CENTER
PATRON FORM

Name _____ Date _____

Address _____

City _____ State _____ ZIP _____ Phone _____

RESEARCH TOPIC:
_____ Genealogy
_____ Civil War
_____ Other _____

PURPOSE OF RESEARCH: (Please add name of group where space is provided.)

_____ Advertising   _____ Publisher   _____ Author
_____ Media   _____ Government   _____ AHC Staff
                       _____ Personal Interest

_____ Business   _____

_____ Organization   _____

_____ Faculty   _____

_____ Student   _____

Instructor's Name   _____

Please return all blue closed stack request forms to reference desk before leaving the library.

I have read the policies of the Atlanta History Center which are listed on the reverse side of this form and hereby agree to conform to them.

SIGNATURE _____

SEE OTHER SIDE PLEASE

1   Deposit with the research assistant briefcases and all other personal property not essential for the work at hand.

2   Smoking is not permitted, and no food or drinks of any kind may be brought into the research room.

3   All materials are to be used with great care. No marks are to be added or removed, and no objects placed on materials. The use of pens, indelible pencils, or felt–tip markers is not permitted under any circumstances. ONLY PENCILS MAY BE USED. No tracings or rubbings are permitted without specific permission.

4   THE EXACT ORDER AND ARRANGEMENT OF THE PAPERS OR MATERIALS MUST BE KEPT INTACT. If any mistake in arrangement is discovered, please call it to the attention of the archivist or librarian. DO NOT REARRANGE PAPERS.

5   In citing these materials, credit must be given to the Atlanta History Center. When preparing material for publication, the researcher is responsible for obtaining the necessary permission from the writer of such documents or his/her literary executer. The researcher must also obtain the written permission for publication from a duly constituted agent of the history center.

6   When finished, please return all materials to the research desk. Books may be left on the tables. DO NOT ATTEMPT TO RESHELVE OR REPLACE MATERIALS.

7   Photo–reproduction (electrostatic copies) will be furnished at the researcher's expense at a cost of $ .25 a sheet. Orders of large quantity will require advance notice. The cost for a rush order of over 30 sheets will be double the aforementioned amount after the first 30 sheets are run. Postage and handling, if required, will be included in the billing.

NOTICE: WARNING CONCERNING COPYRIGHT RESTRICTIONS – The copyright law of the United States (Title 17, U.S. Code) governs the making of photocopies or other reproductions of copyrighted material. Under certain conditions specified in the law, libraries and archives are authorized to furnish a photocopy or other reproduction. One of these specified conditions is that the photocopy or reproduction is not to be "used for any purpose other than private study, scholarship, or research." If a user makes a request for, or later uses, a photocopy or reproduction for purposes in excess of "fair use," that user may be liable for copyright infringement. IT IS THE SOLE RESPONSIBILITY OF THE USER TO OBSERVE ALL COPYRIGHT LAWS.

8   Photographic processing and printing services are available. Check at the reference desk for the schedule and rates.

9   THE RESEARCH MATERIALS OF THE ATLANTA HISTORY CENTER ARE MARKED WITH UNIQUE CHEMICAL COMPOUNDS WHICH, THROUGH SPECTROGRAPHIC ANALYSIS, IDENTIFY THESE MATERIALS AS PROPERTY OF THE CENTER.

    ANY INTENTIONAL MUTILATION, ALTERATION OR DAMAGE TO ANY OF THE RESEARCH MATERIALS OF THE SOCIETY OR THEIR REMOVAL FROM THE PREMISES MAY CONSTITUTE A CRIME UNDER THE LAWS OF GEORGIA, PUNISHABLE BY IMPRISONMENT FOR A PERIOD OF UP TO TEN YEARS. THE CENTER WILL PROSECUTE.

The Atlanta History Center is operated by the Atlanta Historical Society, Inc.

Fig. 4.3b. Patron form, Atlanta History Center. Reprinted with permission of the Atlanta Historical Society, Atlanta, Georgia.

LLMVC
REGULATIONS FOR READERS

Many of the materials in this collection are unique, so we request that you observe these basic rules.

Leave all books, coats, briefcases, purses, etc. in the lobby locker. Personal items in the reading room are subject to search.

When requesting material, present a valid ID and register at the service desk. Legibly complete all forms, including a call slip for each item. Special collections materials do not leave the reading room.

Use only pencils for taking notes. Materials must not be written on, altered, leaned on, folded, traced, or otherwise maltreated. Readers found to be careless or irresponsible in handling materials may be denied further access.

A staff person must be consulted if you wish copies of any materials. Due to physical conditions or special restrictions, some items may not be copied. Compliance with copyright, literary laws and libel rests with the reader.

Any publication of archival and manuscript materials beyond the limits of fair use requires specific prior written permission. Requests for permission to publish should be addressed in writing to the Head, LLMVC.

Proper acknowledgment of materials must be made in any resulting writings or publications. The proper form of citation is the full name of the collection used, followed by "Louisiana and Lower Mississippi Valley Collections, LSU Libraries, Louisiana State University." Copies of scholarly publications based on research in LLMVC are welcomed.

Do not hesitate to ask for assistance from persons at the service desk.

MANUSCRIPT USER REGULATIONS

Many of the materials in this collection are unique, so we request that you observe these basic rules.

Leave all books, coats, briefcases, purses, etc. in the lobby locker. Personal items in the reading room are subject to search.

When requesting material, present a valid ID and register at the service desk. Legibly complete all forms including a call slip for each item. Special collections materials do not leave the reading room.

Use only pencils for taking notes. Materials must not be written on, altered, leaned on, folded, traced, or otherwise maltreated. Readers found to be careless or irresponsible in handling materials may be denied further access.

The existing order and arrangement of unbound materials must be maintained. Apparent irregularities should be reported to the staff member at the desk.

The number of items charged to a reader will be limited in accordance with the nature and condition of materials.

Before segregating items to be copied, consult a Reading Room staff person regarding the proper procedure and pricing. Requests for photoduplication of materials are subject to review and approval on a case by case basis. Permission to copy materials which may be damaged will be denied. Copies of significant portions of collections or series will not be approved. Copies of archival or manuscript materials are provided in lieu of the loan of the originals, strictly for the convenience of the researcher; such copies remain the property of the LSU Libraries and must be returned upon request. The provision of photocopies of archival and manuscript material does not constitute permission to publish.

Any publication of archival and manuscript materials beyond the limits of fair use requires specific prior written permission. Requests for permission to publish should be addressed in writing to the Head, LLMVC.

Proper acknowledgment of materials must be made in any resulting writings or publications. The proper form of citation is the full name of the collection used, followed by "Louisiana and Lower Mississippi Valley Collections, LSU Libraries, Louisiana State University." Copies of scholarly publications based on research in LLMVC are welcomed.

Fig. 4.4. Regulations for readers, Louisiana and Lower Mississippi Valley Collections. Reprinted with permission of the Louisiana and Lower Mississippi Valley Collections, LSU Libraries, Louisiana State University.

Housekeeping

Stacks, shelves, books, and boxes need dusting on a regular basis. Floors in all areas need regular cleaning. Dust accumulates in even the cleanest environment. If the library does not have regular custodians, staff members and volunteers should be asked to help. If all staff do small parts of the cleaning, everyone and everything in the local history collection will benefit, and no one is likely to resent this assignment.

Lighting Controls

Light creates preservation problems. It causes discoloration and fading and breaks down the fibers in the paper. Therefore, staff must turn off stack lights, except when materials are being retrieved. This means, of course, that permanent work spaces cannot be placed in stack areas. With low budgets, limited space, and overcrowding, work space must sometimes be established in a stack area, but this should be temporary. Windows in stack areas are not advisable. If windows exist in the stack areas, cover them. All lights in the stacks, in the work areas, and in the reading room of the local history collection should have ultraviolet light shields.[3]

The most dangerous light of all, however, is the light in photocopy machines. Twentieth century Americans have an uncommon love affair with photocopiers. The proliferation of photocopies makes the job of the archivist even more complicated, because of the increase in paper and the appraisal difficulties inherent in multiple copies. But the greatest harm of all comes from photocopying items. The intense heat and light needed to make a photocopy breaks down paper fiber, discolors it, and generally shortens its life. Photocopiers with moving or flat tops do great damage to books by breaking their spines and shaking them. Placing any book with a tight spine on a photocopier with a flat copying surface will eventually break its spine. Photocopying of rare printed materials, manuscripts, and archives must be severely limited. Staff members can encourage researchers to take notes from these materials. It is the staff's job to gently, but firmly, teach researchers to respect holdings and not ask for excessive copies. Diplomacy benefits both sides.

Insect Damage Controls

The second most prevalent problem is insects. Bad storage creates hospitable environments for insects and vermin. Materials coming into the local history collection with evidence of insects must be fumigated. Freezing is the least harmful method, because no chemicals are involved. The Louisiana and Lower Mississippi Valley Collections uses a freezer to kill insects and insect eggs on paper. A large walk-in freezer (originally designed for meat storage) is used to freeze all books and paper materials that show evidence of insect infestation. The items are boxed; bagged in large, black garbage bags; and placed in the freezer for 24 to 48 hours at a temperature of -30 degrees. After this time, the items are removed from the freezer and allowed to return slowly to room temperature over the next 48 hours. They are then unbagged, unboxed, and dusted. Caution should be taken not to freeze items that can be damaged such as photographs, wood, plastics, some cloths, glass, and leather. Small household freezers may be used for the same purpose, if they are frost-free. Freezers and refrigerators used for food storage by people must never be used for freezing materials infested with insects. If the library has a freezer or refrigerator for staff use, it must be in an entirely different area of the library. The freezer used for infested materials must be clearly marked with warning labels that no food is allowed.

Many libraries and local history collections have invested substantial sums in providing fumigation chambers that use chemicals. These vacuum fumigation chambers have in the past used the chemicals ethylene oxide and thymol. Both are very dangerous to people. Libraries should contact their state archives or library or large university libraries for assistance in selecting fumigating materials. It is not recommended that small local history collections invest in fumigation chambers because of their danger. Photographs should never be placed in any type of chemical fumigate. To control insects in the collection, it is recommended that a commercial pest control service be used, if the service can show proof that its chemicals have not caused adverse reactions in humans. Commercial companies use a variety of chemicals to prevent the insects from building up an immunity to any one, but illnesses have been reported by staff exposed to chemicals in some areas. Caution must be exercised.[4]

Microfilming for Preservation

Once insects are controlled, other conservation or preservation methods may be needed for local history collection materials. Microfilming is an excellent way to preserve manuscripts, archives, and rare printed materials. However, manuscripts and archives microfilmed without proper arrangement and description may be impossible to use. In such cases, microfilming is of no help in preservation, for the originals will still need to be consulted. Once items are microfilmed, researchers' use of the film will prevent continued wear on the original items. Copies may also be made from microfilm with the use of a microfilm reader printer. Microfiche may also be used, but 35mm silver halide microfilm is the archival preference because of its quality and durability.

An in-house microfilming program requires trained staff and proper equipment.[5] Microfilm cameras are expensive and require substantial workspace that can be darkened as needed. Microfiche, 35mm planetary cameras, and rotary cameras are available from Kodak, 3-M, and other companies, but caution is necessary in acquiring equipment. The library should be certain the cameras are warranted and that training is included in the contract. Is a maintenance contract available at a reasonable rate? What is the track record of the equipment regarding repairs? Talk with someone who has purchased this type of equipment and has been using it for several years. How long has the company been in business and manufacturing microfilm cameras? Will the company process the microfilm at a reasonable rate and in a timely manner? Will the company guarantee that it follows American National Standards Institute (ANSI) standards in processing the film? Staff should make a list of other questions to be asked of all salespeople and see representatives of several different companies. If the library must purchase items on the bid system, be sure the specifications are written carefully to insure the acquisition of the camera that is best for the collection. An in-house microfilming program is not recommended unless the library has substantial funding for equipment and the required trained staff. Also, the library should have an ongoing commitment to maintaining the microfilming program at the highest possible standards.

Libraries planning in-house microfilming programs must also make a decision about processing. Processing equipment is as expensive as microfilm cameras and requires an even greater investment in staff training. Kodak and other companies will process microfilm for libraries and archives at a reasonable fee and do archival quality work. Again, be certain that any company guarantees that it follows ANSI standards. Many state libraries and archives have microfilming labs and will contract to process microfilm for other libraries. Such contract services are an excellent way to have film processed and are less expensive than an in-house lab. Two copies of the film are required, a negative and a positive. Only positive film is made available for the use of researchers. Negative film is the master copy. Negative film is much like a photograph negative; once the negative is destroyed, no more copies of the photograph or microfilm can be made without producing another negative. Negative microfilm scratches easily and must be used only in an emergency to produce extra positive copies. The negative film, the security copy, is stored off-site. Some state archives have microfilm storage vaults and will make space available to local libraries. Some commercial companies also rent archival storage space, but caution should be taken and a sound investigation conducted before using a commercial storage firm. If a disaster occurs at the local history collection, the microfilm negatives stored off-site can be used to replace damaged positive microfilm.

Many libraries also contract out microfilming. Again, some state archives and state and university libraries do microfilming for other institutions on a contract basis. Many state and local governments have established microfilming programs in prisons on a cost recovery basis. Materials, of course, must be taken to the prison for filming, but many governments have found this a practical solution to the problem of microfilming government records. Information on such programs may be available from the state archives or the state records management division. As with any contract service, caution must be taken to ensure the safety and careful handling of the materials being microfilmed. Before contracting with any agency to do microfilming of nonreplaceable items or items on loan to the local history collection, visit the lab, talk with the staff, and ask to see all procedures and policies in writing. How will the materials be picked up and returned? Where will they be stored while waiting to be microfilmed? Is the work area of the contracting agency clean, safe, and secure? Is there danger of theft of the materials? Is food allowed in the microfilming area? Are all procedures up to archival and ANSI standards?[6]

Once the decision is made to microfilm materials, proper procedures for identifying and handling the materials must be established. Books and other printed materials being microfilmed need identifying target sheets—pages of information inserted before microfilming at the beginning of the film, stating who owns the material and who is doing the microfilming. Other target sheets state copyright restrictions, microfilming standards used to make the film, and other necessary restrictions or comments. If pages are missing or damaged, a target sheet should be inserted to show this. Before microfilming, manuscripts and archives staff should arrange and describe them, and a copy of the finding aid (inventory) should be microfilmed with the materials at the beginning of the film. After printed materials are microfilmed, the production of the microfilm master (the negative) should be reported to the National Register of Microform Masters of the Library of Congress (*Microfilm Masters* is also available on RLIN). Before producing microfilm of a book, consult *Microform Masters* to determine whether a film already exists. Most of these microforms are available for purchase at a lower cost than microfilming the item again. Microfilms of manuscripts and archives should be reported to *National Union Catalog of Manuscript Collections* (*NUCMC*) and to national databases.

For local history collections that cannot afford an in-house microfilming program or commercial microfilming, some help can be received from other institutions. The Church of Jesus Christ of Latter-Day Saints has an extensive microfilm program. Staff of the church travel throughout the United States microfilming materials they feel will be helpful to their church members' genealogical research. LDS Church members film on-site and follow the rules and regulations of the library they are visiting. There is no charge to the local history collection. Staff should contact the LDS Church in Salt Lake City, Utah, for information.[7] Local institutions may have microfilming programs that the local history collection can utilize.

What should be microfilmed? Among other items, materials borrowed from donors for microfilming only, printed materials too fragile to be handled by researchers, manuscripts and archives that receive extensive photocopying and borrowing requests, and books that patrons from other libraries have requested. No matter what is to be microfilmed, careful evaluation of the need to microfilm and the cost to microfilm must be considered.

Document Preservation

Even with limited resources a local history collection can perform document preservation tasks, which will help preserve the materials and do no damage to them. Humidifying, deacidifying, and encapsulating documents; sleeving and rephotographing photographs; oiling book bindings; and rehousing projects must be the first priorities of local history collections. One staff member should be trained in these techniques and then be placed in charge of any preservation work to be done in the department. Nearby archives, libraries, or universities may have training programs for staff or be willing to share their expertise on a one-to-one basis.

Again, a staff member in charge of basic preservation should establish a work area designated exclusively for such work. Supplies need to be kept in the work area and used only by the preservation staff. Administrators should set aside some of the supplies budget each year to buy special materials (see fig. 4.5). Staff in charge of preservation should keep careful records of all work done on materials. Books to be repaired, microfilmed, or oiled are checked out to the appropriate staff member and a detailed worksheet kept on all activities that take place (see fig. 4.6, on page 68). The staff should keep a log listing when materials are received, what is to be done, when the work was begun, and when completed (see fig. 4.7, on page 69). Manuscripts and archives for preservation work are also checked out to the appropriate staff member, who keeps a worksheet on all procedures. The rule of thumb for basic preservation work is *"Never do anything that cannot be undone."* Encapsulation of a document can be undone, lamination cannot. If the damage to an item is severe and needs very special work, the best thing to do is house it properly, limit research use, forbid copying, and do nothing else unless special funds can be acquired to send the item to professional conservators. The Society of American Archivists has published a directory listing conservators and other qualified consultants.[8]

Staff members should follow a preservation procedures checklist while handling preliminary processing. As materials are received, staff can route items for preservation to the correct staff along with an appropriate worksheet. In this way, preservation is done on a daily basis and the backlog is minimized.

white cotton gloves	acid-free blotting paper
rustproof paper clips	nonbuffered acid-free folders for
acid-free bond paper	photographs
acid-free folders and boxes	Mylar photograph sleeves
phase box acid-free board	burnishing bone
Mylar	microspatulas
soft-bristle brushes	dry-cleaning pad
encapsulation kit	small vacuum cleaner
Wei T'o Deacidification Solution	

Fig. 4.5. Basic preservation supplies.

Text continues on page 70.

PRELIMINARY PROCESSING REPORT

Name of collection:

Accession #:   Manuscript group #:
                                                  Record group #:

Date received:

INSTRUCTIONS

1. Refer to the Processing Manual for general instructions. Follow specific instructions below.

2. Be sure to keep track of your time on verso of this form.

3. Complete Preservation Log form as you work.

4. When you have finished preliminary processing, ask your supervisor to review your work.

5. Type a container list as directed by your supervisor.

SPECIFIC INSTRUCTIONS FOR THIS COLLECTION:

Processed by: Date completed:

Location in stacks: Shelved by:

Size:

Description:

Fig. 4.6. Preliminary processing report. Reprinted with permission of the Louisiana and Lower Mississippi Valley Collections, LSU Libraries, Louisiana State University.

PRESERVATION LOG

Collection Name: _____   Manuscript Group #: _____

Processor: _____   Record Group #: _____

Collection date range: _____

Container types: _____

Type of Materials (check as appropriate)
_____ Manuscript sheets   _____ Plain paper copies
_____ Typescript   _____ Carbon copies
_____ Computer papers   _____ Other copies
_____ Oversize   _____ Printed materials
_____ Woodpulp   _____ Scrapbook
_____ Parchment   _____ Seals or ribbons
_____ Colored inks   _____ Photographic images

Condition Problems (check as appropriate)
_____ Mold damage   _____ Staples, clips, pins
_____ Insect damage   _____ Rubber bands
_____ Mildew   _____ Tape
_____ Surface dirt   _____ Fragile
_____ Folded/rolled   _____ Torn, broken
_____ Fire damage   _____ Stains
_____ Water damage   _____ Glues, adhesives
_____ Faded writing   _____ Other (specify)

To Be Done (check as appropriate)
_____ Freeze   _____ Copy (acid-free paper)
_____ Staple, clip, pin removal _____ Interleave
_____ Humidify, flatten   _____ Refolder
_____ Dryclean   _____ Rebox
_____ Move to oversize   *_____ Send to conservation
_____ Sleeve photographs

*All requests for deacidification, tape removal, or other chemical procedures
MUST be referred to the conservation department.

Comments:

Fig. 4.7. Preservation log. Reprinted with permission of the Louisiana and Lower
Mississippi Valley Collections, LSU Libraries, Louisiana State University.

Preservation Requirements Survey

Local history collections tend, however, to have backlogs of materials needing preservation. Gauge the collection problems and needs by having the staff complete a preservation needs survey. Begin by determining what is to be accomplished by the survey. Will the survey review rehousing needs, such as new folders and new boxes? Will it identify only printed materials in need of small repairs or microfilming because of fragility? Or will it identify manuscripts and archival materials in need of encapsulation, deacidification, and other work? How extensive will the survey be, and what is the time framework? A survey form is needed to track information for later input into a computer (see fig. 4.8).

FIELD SURVEY
CONDITION NOTES

Collection:

Donor: Location:

Estimated size:
    boxed   loose
    filing cabinets   other

Special formats/condition:

        Description   Amount   Location

Water damage:

Mold or insect infestation:

Packing supplies: Special equipment:

Approx. # of packing days: Personnel:

Transportation:

Additional comments:

Archivist _____ Date _____

Fig. 4.8. Sample field survey form that incorporates condition notes and special handling instructions. From Mary Lynn Ritzenthaler, *Archives and Manuscripts: Conservation* (Chicago: Society of American Archivists, 1983), 49. Reprinted with permission of the Society of American Archivists.

One staff member designated as the team leader can appoint a team to do the survey and to adhere to a time limit. Results of the survey can then be reviewed by all staff members.

After completing the survey, plan procedures for the preservation staff to begin work on the findings. Such work can take place simultaneously with preservation work on newly received materials. In this way, the backlog of preservation needs can be completed.[9]

The Disaster Plan

Daily maintenance and preservation of the local history collection will provide for long life of the materials, if disasters do not occur. If disasters, manmade or natural, do occur, a well-thought-out disaster plan can rescue the collection. A disaster plan is "the policies and procedures intended to prevent or minimize damage to archival materials resulting from disasters."[10] Disasters can be fires, floods, or thefts. Any number of problems can be caused by natural events, such as hurricanes and earthquakes.

Disaster plans include procedures for securing damaged buildings and materials, and the names and phone numbers of police, fire, ambulance services, companies with proper freezer and fumigation equipment, and library administrators. They also include steps to follow regarding removal of damaged materials from the building, freeze-drying of water damaged items, insurance claims, and work plans for staff during recovery. Other important information includes the names of insurance agents, contractors for repair work, and news media. All staff require training regarding disasters and copies of the disaster plans. Disasters cannot always be avoided; therefore, planning for recovery from them is the next best approach.[11]

Carefully acquired, thoroughly cataloged, properly housed, and adequately secured materials provide optimum conditions for continuing research use of the local history collection.

Notes

1. Timothy Walch, *Archives and Manuscripts: Security* (Chicago: Society of American Archivists, 1977), 1-30.

2. Some excellent preservation guides are: Mary Lynn Ritzenthaler, *Archives and Manuscripts: Conservation* (Chicago: Society of American Archivists, 1983); Mary L. Ritzenthaler, Gerald Munoff, and Margery S. Long, *Archives and Manuscripts: Administration of Photographic Collections*; "Special Preservation Issue," *American Archivist* 53 (1990). Other readings on preservation can be found in the annual bibliography on archives in the *American Archivist*.

3. For further information on proper work spaces and the problems of light see: George Cunha and Dorothy Cunha, *Library and Archives Conservation*:

1980's and Beyond, 2 vols. (Metuchen, NJ: Scarecrow Press, 1983). An excellent and understandable discussion of how paper is created, why acid deterioration exists, how light affects paper, and how to protect papers can be found in *Archival Storage Materials and Conservation Supplies Catalogue* (Springfield, VA: Conservation Resources International, 1988), 2-13. Phone 703-321-7730, 800-634-6932, or FAX 703-321-0629.

4. Cunha and Cunha, *Library and Archives Conservation.*

5. Nancy E. Gwinn, ed., *Preservation Microfilming: A Guide for Librarians and Archivists* (Chicago: American Library Association, 1987); Janet E. Gertz, "Preservation Microfilming for Archives and Manuscripts," *American Archivist* 53 (1990): 224-235.

6. Gwinn, *Preservation Microfilming*, 175-177. ANSI is the American National Standards Institute, 1430 Broadway, New York, NY 10018, 212-354-3300.

7. Genealogical Society of Utah, 50 East North Temple Street, Salt Lake City, UT 84150, 801-531-2298.

8. *Directory of Consultants* (Chicago: Society of American Archivists, 1992).

9. The National Association of Government Archives and Records Administrators (NAGARA) has developed a *Guide and Resources for Archives Strategic Preservation Planning* (GRASP) (Lexington, KY: Council of State Governments, 1992). GRASP has three interrelated tools, the Computer Assisted Self-Study, the Manual, and the Resource Compendium. Information on NAGARA GRASP can be obtained form the NAGARA Office, Council of State Governments, Iron Works Pike, P.O. Box 11910, Lexington, KY 40578. See also: Bonnie Rose Curtin, "Preservation Planning for Archives: Development and Field Testing of the NAGARA GRASP," *American Archivist* 53 (1990): 236-243.

10. Lewis J. Bellardo and Lynn Lady Bellardo, comps., *A Glossary for Archivists, Manuscript Curators, and Records Managers* (Chicago: Society of American Archivists, 1992), 11.

11. For helpful information on disaster planning see: Priscilla O'Reilly Lawrence, *Before Disaster Strikes: Prevention, Planning, and Recovery* (New Orleans: The Historic New Orleans Collection, 1992). Contact the Historic New Orleans Collection, 504-523-4662, FAX 504-522-5108. Repair information is available in: BookLab, *BookNote 2: Salvage of Library Materials from Water or Insect Damage* (Austin, TX: BookLab, Inc., not dated). Contact BookLab, Inc., 8403 Cross Park Drive, Suite 2-E, Austin, TX 78754, 512-837-0479, FAX 512-837-9794. Cunha and Cunha, *Library and Archives Conservation*; and Peter Waters, *Emergency Procedures for Salvaging Flood or Water Damaged Library Materials*, 2d ed. (Washington, DC: Library of Congress, 1979).

5 New Technologies for Access and Preservation

Although microfilming has long been the mainstay of technology for access and preservation of library and archival materials, there are now new technologies emerging for improving access and preservation. Optical scanners, compact disc-read only memory (CD-ROM), multimedia computer interactive programs, videotape, scanner/copiers that reproduce facsimile books, and advanced computer databases and programs are some of the advanced technologies available to librarians, archivists, and the users of local history collections.[1]

Some of these technologies are too expensive and too high-tech for small to medium-sized local history collections and their parent libraries. But many are within reach of even the smallest collections and can be used to aid all researchers from high school students to scholars. Many current projects serve as models for what local history collections can do to broaden access and use and add more information to their collections.

Fiber Optics

The development of laser light by Theodor Maiman in 1960 led to fiber optics technology that makes it possible to transmit enormous amounts of data through digital communication systems. CD-ROMs and videodiscs use lasers and digital data. Voice, image text, and data can also be sent through telephone lines to local computer systems. This technology allows a convergence of computing, audio, video, printing and publishing, and communications. "One result of this could be to make local studies more truly 'local,' so that the history of a community could be researched in that community without the need for lengthy and expensive journeys to county town or capital city."[2] Such technology is the basis on which true libraries without walls can be built.

American Memory Project

One of the most exciting and noteworthy projects in this area is the Library of Congress's American Memory Project. According to James H. Billington, Librarian of Congress, the American Memory Project "constitutes a first step in the library's long-term effort to share our collections—especially primary source holdings—via technology with local library users from Maine to California."[3]

American Memory, with the use of CD-ROMs and laser videodiscs, make primary source materials from the Library of Congress available for researchers, teachers, students, and the public in local and school libraries. The program is available online as well. Users have access to collections such as Documents of the Continental Congress and Constitutional Convention, 1774-1789; Paper Print Films of New York City, 1897-1906; Early Sound Recordings from America's Leaders, 1918-1920; African-American Pamphlets, 1820-1920; and Civil War Photographs, 1861-1865. The collections are accompanied by interpretive introductions, guides for users, and bibliographies for further research. The advanced technology used in the American Memory program will "offer new and novel ways of using primary source materials." Searching can be done electronically through entire collections to find information on specific topics. Users can "electronically copy" content for use at other locations. This means a researcher can locate text and images, copy them onto a floppy disk, and take the information home to use. This will also "enable researchers to collect primary materials, teachers to prepare classroom handouts, or students to do primary research for homework assignments."[4]

Workstations for American Memory require a microcomputer, a CD-ROM player, a videodisc player and a video monitor. The CD-ROM discs have a master catalog that is composed of MARC-like bibliographic records. These records offer a broad overview and more "specific indexes and bodies of free text (machine-readable texts) that offer detailed access to individual collections." Data records text are seen on the computer screen, and photographs and moving images are seen on the television monitor. CD-ROMs are digital and videodiscs contain analog video signals. Textual documents or manuscript pages are viewable as facsimiles or as conversions of the printed text. Facsimiles are produced by scanning, and printed text is presented in a machine-readable form by either typing the information into the program or by scanning and doing automated optical character recognition. Scanners cannot yet read handwriting, so manuscripts appear only as pictures of the pages. In some cases, variant forms of interactive compact discs as well as still-frame-audio-on-television videodiscs are used.

> Some visual collections will be in the form of analog video. Although lower in resolution than the digitized images, analog video offers a very satisfactory presentation of such items as photographs. A single side of a 12-inch analog videodisc can contain more than 50,000 images. Sections of text or visual items can be printed directly or sent to the program's "workshop."

The workshop will offer a way to transfer saved images and text into word-processing or "desktop publishing" documents. Digitized images and texts are immediately available; video images will first be digitized by a video frame conversion device ("frame grabber"). The workshop will allow users to assemble all types of images into onscreen presentation similar to slide shows.[5]

Local and Regional Databases

Many local history collections have their own versions of the American Memory project. The Western History Collections at the University of Oklahoma is planning a project to create a CD-ROM of a full-text database containing printed materials, handwritten manuscripts, color photographs, maps, posters, and audio recordings on the subjects of Native Americans, Westward Expansion, and Oklahoma history. The Louisiana and Lower Mississippi Valley Collections' Electronic Imaging Laboratory has published a CD-ROM edition of B. F. French's *Historical Collections of Louisiana, Embracing Many Rare and Valuable Documents Related to the Natural, Civil and Political History of That State*, first published in five volumes by Wiley and Putnam of New York beginning in 1846. The CD-ROM contains a full text that is keyword searchable and includes maps and facsimile pages of the original texts. Facsimile pages and maps are accessible through a hypertext system developed by IBM. The volumes were scanned and then read with Kurzweil, Inc. optical character recognition systems (a subsidiary of Xerox) and then edited in WordPerfect. The CD-ROM edition sells for about $50.[6]

Commercial Systems

While the scanning and video projects of the Library of Congress, the Western History Collections, and the Louisiana and Lower Mississippi Valley Collections are extremely expensive ones, ranging from hundreds of thousands to millions of dollars, the ability to scan, digitize, and provide broader access to local history collection materials is available at minimal costs. Numerous companies have developed software programs and hardware equipment that the local history collection can afford in order to provide more information to their users.

The Typist Plus Graphics, a product of Caere, is advertised as the ultimate typing machine. It is a low-cost (around $300), hand-held scanner designed for OCR (optical character recognition). As the text is scanned, it is recognized and then appears directly in a word-processing application. The Typist Plus Graphics is also used for scanning photographs and other images, and it can do image-editing. With the addition of Caere's Graphic Editor and LaserGray technology, the images can be printed.

Caere is also the maker of OmniPage Direct, an easy-to-use OCR software for accurate text recognition (around $300). It can add OCR directly to Windows or Macintosh word-processing, spreadsheet, desktop publishing, or communications software. Although it does not do graphics or images, it can read in eleven European languages.

Other scanners range from the low priced Complete PC (around $600) to Epson's ES-300C Color Scanner (around $900). The Complete PC page scanner with Calera's WordScan OCR software and SmartScan software can scan photographs, art, logos, text, and graphics for editing in word-processing software. The Epson can scan up to 16.7 million different colors and can be used with the Hewlett-Packard PaintJet to print directly, but this requires added software. There is also Panasonic's FX-RS506U OCR scanner (around $900), which includes ReadRight OCR software or Calera's WordScan for Macintosh and Windows.

Another hand-held scanner is Logitech Scanman with Perceive Personal OCR software (around $350) which can "stitch" together two, three, or four scans using Virtual Page Scanning with Logitech Autostitching features to automatically merge scans into one completely seamless image or text page. It also comes in ScanMan Color (around $400), which is the first handscanner to use 24-bit color scanning, or CatchWord Pro OCR software (around $300). This software automatically stitches together and merges the necessary multiple scans for image or text wider than four inches.

Apple OneScanner for the Macintosh has Ofoto one-step imaging-scanning software. It is a flatbed scanner and is primarily intended for imaging. Ofoto first scans the picture at low resolution, then rescans it at high resolution, automatically adjusting for brightness and contrast. The scanner can be used with Caere's OmniPage Direct OCR software. The Ofoto software is available separately (around $300) and works with other scanners such as the Hewlett-Packard ScanJet. For a few thousand dollars, Apple personal computer systems with interactive audiovideo, scanning and OCR, desktop publishing, CD-ROM players, and numerous software programs can be purchased for the local history collection.[7]

In order to make the scanned images of photographs or other materials from the local history collection usable by staff and patrons, indexes are still needed. Scanned images can be indexed through computer software such as dBase or Shareware using programs like "Organize Your Photos and Slides." A new product is ImagePals software, which contains a 24-bit image editor, a screen-capture utility, and an image manager and viewer. The capture works only with Windows programs, but will capture any portion of the screen to a work space or to a file and name any number of files consecutively using personal file name specifications. The Album image manager and viewer module make it possible to view thumbnail versions of the images in a low-resolution copy of the original, which is stored in the file format chosen, from TIFF to the compression format JPEG. The thumbnail image can be clicked on to get file information such as size, date created, and notes—then it can be enlarged. The Enhancer opens the files for editing.

Finally, Kodak has developed a Photo CD system that uses film and electronic imaging. The system captures a picture from film, digitizes it with a scanner, and stores it on a compact disc. The disc drive can display the picture on a television screen, manipulate it on a computer, merge it with documents, or print it out on a digital color printer. Scanners such as those from Apple work with the Kodak system.

Like microfilm, these technologies allow local history collections to reformat manuscripts, photographs, and rare printed materials to reduce use of the originals. By reformatting, wear and tear on the original materials is reduced. Also, the reformatted version of materials may be loanable through interlibrary loan, whereas the originals would not be. Projects such as the reformatting of brittle books at Cornell University not only rescue books that are unusable, but make it possible for local history collections to purchase facsimiles of those books at a reasonable price. True, none of these technologies take the place of conservation of original materials but they do broaden access, which is one of the main concerns of local history collections.[8]

The transmission of local history collection information is most familiar in the national online databases of OCLC and RLIN. Records of materials in the local history collection are available to any user of OCLC and RLIN anywhere in the world. Items located can be borrowed through interlibrary loan. RLIN also includes the records for the National Union Catalog of Manuscript Collections (NUCMC). Any local history collection can submit descriptive entries for their cataloged manuscript collections for entry by the Library of Congress into RLIN. OCLC also has entries for manuscript collections from local history collections. Researchers may purchase individual accounts to search on RLIN (see chapter 3 for a discussion of cataloging on OCLC and RLIN).

Computer and Fax

Computer networks have also made electronic mail (e-mail) available to local history collections and their researchers. Reference inquiries can be made through modem hookup (with telephone lines) to systems such as Bitnet and Internet. CompuServe and Prodigy are online computer services for personal computers that allow researchers to purchase access to e-mail systems. Patrons can now e-mail a request for information to connected local history collections and probably receive an answer the same way. Fax (facsimile transmission) also allows researchers and staff of local history collections to query other collections more efficiently and quickly than through the mail and eases the difficulties in reaching someone by telephone. Fax is also transmitted via telephone lines.[9]

Personal computers are being used more and more by the staff of local history collections and their patrons. Many computer programs are available for use by genealogical researchers. *Genealogical and Local History Books in Print*, compiled by Netti Schreiner-Yantis (4th edition 1985, and supplements 1990) from Genealogical Books in Print, Springfield, VA, lists companies that provide such software. The *Directory of Genealogical Software: Your Guide to the Genealogy Software Market Today* is available through Ancestry Inc., P.O. Box 476, 350 South 400 East, Suite 110, Salt Lake City, UT 84110, and includes names and addresses of vendors, prices, system requirements, and descriptions of the software. A useful new newsletter is *Computer Genealogy Notebook*, 1104 Carroll Drive, Garland, TX 75041.

Because of the high cost of computer software, the Association of Shareware Professionals was developed. Vendors of Shareware allow the buyer to evaluate computer programs for around $3.50 per disk. Users are allowed to try out the software, thereby eliminating the risk of purchasing software that does not work for a particular need. If the buyer decides to keep the software, a fee of $15 to $100 is charged. One such program is "Brother's Keeper 5.1," which tracks up to one million people and is advertised as an easy-to-use, state of the art genealogy program. It generates descendant charts, ancestor charts, family group sheets, alphabetical name lists, descendant trees, birthday lists, box charts, and customized reports.[10]

While these products, concepts, and computer software programs are just a few of the new technologies available, they typify the variety available to local history collections for expanding their services. As such technologies continue to develop, local history collections can truly become libraries without walls.

Notes

1. M. Stuart Lynn, *Preservation and Access Technology, the Relationship Between Digital and Other Media Conversion Processes: A Structured Glossary of Technical Terms* (Washington, DC: The Commission on Preservation and Access, 1990).

2. Mike Seton, "Information Technology," *Local Studies Collections: A Manual, Volume 2*, Michael Dewe, ed. (Hants, England: Gower Publishing, 1991), 137-138.

3. James H. Billington, "Library of Congress to Open Collections to Local Libraries in Electronic Access Plans," *American Libraries* 22 (1991): 706.

4. "American Memory from the Library of Congress: A Catalog of Collections in Preparation and Under Consideration" (Washington, DC: Library of Congress, 1991), 1. For more information contact American Memory, Special Projects, Library of Congress, Washington, DC 20540, 202-707-6233.

5. *LC Information Bulletin* (February 26, 1990): 87.

6. For information, contact the Western History Collections, University Libraries, University of Oklahoma, 630 Parrington Oval, Room 452, Norman, OK 73019; and the Louisiana and Lower Mississippi Valley Collections, Louisiana State University, Hill Memorial Library, Baton Rouge, LA 70803, 504-388-6568, FAX 504-388-6992. The CD-ROM is available from the Louisiana State University Press.

7. The listing of a product in this chapter in no way is meant to serve as an endorsement. The listings are only to provide examples of new technology. Information on individual products can be acquired from the manufacturer or from mail order computer companies such as Lyben Computer Systems, 5545 Bridgewood, Sterling Heights, MI 48310, 313-268-8100, FAX 313-268-8899; or Elek-Tek, Inc., 7350 N. Linder Ave., Skokie, IL 60077, 800-395-1000, FAX 708-677-7168.

8. For information on the Brittle Books project write the Commission on Preservation and Access, 1400 16th Street, NW, Suite 740, Washington, DC 20036-2217.

9. See the *Directory to Fulltext Online Resources 1992* (Westport, CT: Meckler, 1992), which can be obtained from Meckler Publishing, 11 Ferry Lane W., Westport, CT 06880.

10. One such company is Reasonable Solutions, 1221 Disk Drive, Medford, OR 97501, phone 503-776-5777, FAX 503-773-7803.

The Users of Local History Collections

The type of institution in which the local history collection exists determines who are the most frequent users. Patrons or users include scholars, club members, students from grade school through post-graduate, businesspeople, politicians, amateur and professional historians, amateur and professional genealogists, historic preservations, playwrights, and almost every other member of the community.

The primary users of university and college libraries are students and faculty of the school. Other users may be visiting scholars, staff members of the school, and administrators. Citizens of the town will also use the local history collection in the university library. Research may range from term papers to dissertations to scholarly books for university presses.

Public libraries serve everyone in the community. Thus the local history collection of a public library also serves all community members, making the needs of the collection broader and more diverse than those in college libraries. Of course, users of university and college libraries and public libraries are interchangeable. The only difference in clientele may be grade school children, who do not often visit university and college libraries.

Special libraries such as private research libraries, business libraries, hospital libraries, and government agency libraries hold materials identified with local history. Special libraries exist for the employees of businesses, hospitals, and government and may not be open to the public without permission. However, in order to fill the needs of their users, special libraries will acquire materials about the area in which they are located. Private research libraries, such as the Henry E. Huntington Library and Art Gallery in California, are used by scholars who apply in advance to do research there. Casual visits to private research libraries are permissible only to take advantage of public tours.

Historical society libraries are usually local history collections with special reference materials for society staff, which are often open to the public on either a regular schedule or by appointment. Large historical society libraries offer the user full reference and research services. Small historical society libraries have few professional staff and only limited access to their local history collection materials. Researchers should write or telephone before visiting a historical society library to determine its hours and the requirements for use.[1]

Museums may also house extensive local history collections. These assist curators in preparing exhibitions about the local area. Many museums make their materials available to the public by appointment, even though they seldom have librarians or archivists on staff.

Access

Local history collections that are open to the public should have an equal access policy. Equal access implies that a repository of research materials will make these materials available to all users on an equal basis. No researcher will be given preferential access over others.[2] The Society of American Archivists has adopted "Standards for Access to Research Materials in Archival and Manuscripts Repositories."[3]

The use policy of the local history collection identifies who may use it. Included are registration requirements and the types of restrictions on use. The statement may be included in the collection development policy, brochures, patron rules, and other handouts. The policy must be made available to all researchers.

The local history collection can best serve users by having a central, continually staffed reference desk where users ask questions and receive assistance. Staff should never leave the reading room unattended. Tables and all work areas in the reading room should be arranged so that they are clearly visible by a staff member at all times. Staff who learn to monitor the activities in the reading area systematically, and who accept the responsibility for enforcing rules, improve security.[4] It is very important to know the location of closed stack materials at all times. Many universities and colleges are fortunate to have student workers who perform the tasks of retrieving and reshelving materials in the stacks. Other libraries may not have this luxury, and therefore, regular staff assume these duties. Scheduled rotation of reference and retrieval duties helps balance the fatigue associated with these responsibilities. All staff should be exposed to reference duties in order to better understand the purposes of preparing the materials for use.

All libraries face the problems of lost, stolen, destroyed, and worn items. In order to maintain a permanent collection and minimize problems, local history collections use the special controls of registration, security, and restricted access. The department should require each patron to complete a registration form and to present photo identification before they are allowed to use any materials from the closed stacks. In addition, the staff should give each new patron a list of user rules that they may keep. The researcher acknowledges by signing the registration form that he or she has read the rules and agrees to abide by them (see chapter 3 for reader regulations and sample registration forms). User regulations give the basic rules for using materials in the department, information on photocopying, proper citation for materials quoted from the collection, how to ask for permission to publish, and items (e.g., pens, typewriters, and computers) that may or may not be used in the reading room. Staff must answer any questions regarding these rules politely and thoroughly.

Registration forms completed by researchers increase security. Update forms at least once every two years and keep them in active files for five years and in inactive files for 20 years. Some collections keep these files permanently. The registration forms serve three purposes: statistical, informational, and as a detriment to theft. Statistics developed from the forms show how many people are using the collection and when. Information gathered by reviewing the forms shows the topics researchers are working on so that staff may inform appropriate users when new materials relating to their topics are received. Local history collections that require identification and reader registration have fewer thefts than those that do not. Such registration and other security procedures are not meant to imply that users of local history collections are potential thieves, but to help protect materials that have high monetary value. Such items may attract professional thieves. Required registration and tight security measures can deter thieves, professional and amateur. The Rare Book and Manuscripts Section of the Association of College and Research Libraries have developed "Guidelines for the security of rare book, manuscripts, and other special collections," which aid in planning security measures for local history collections.[5]

Other vital security measures include requiring patrons to leave all types of bags including purses and handbags, briefcases, backpacks, school books, and other noncollection materials in lockers with security locks. Local history collection researchers may have notepads, notecards, pencils, or computers but nothing else while doing work in the collection's reading room. This policy is another deterrent to theft and to possible mix-ups when local history collection materials are inadvertently removed from the reading room.

Staff, regular or part-time, assist security of the local history collection by wearing identification badges at all times. Only personnel with badges are allowed in the stacks, and patrons are always aware who staff members are. It is also helpful to have researchers using the local history collection wear visitor badges. This adds another level of security. Some special collections issue researcher cards to patrons that they use as identification when asking for materials. Once every two years, a new card is issued and researcher registration forms are updated.

Despite the best intentions of staff and administration, some patrons will disagree with the rules of the local history collection. Some will simply voice objections and then agree to follow the rules, but others will refuse to accept them. When this problem occurs, staff must firmly but gently insist that the rules be followed before a patron is allowed to use materials. If a patron is rude to staff or loud and disruptive, call the administrator or security personnel to talk with them. Attempt to get the disruptive person to leave the reading room, so that other patrons will not be disturbed. Be polite, firm, and diplomatic. The staff's objective should be to keep one individual from disturbing all others using the collection. The staff should attempt to answer complaints without compromising the security of the collection. If all attempts fail to calm the person, he or she should be asked to leave the library and should be escorted out by security personnel or, if necessary, the police.

Security for the local history collection will be a real problem unless the department has a closed stack area separate from other collections of the library. Closed stack arrangements are impossible in many libraries due to the design of the building or space limitations. If print materials cannot be secured in a closed stack, perhaps the stacks where local history collection materials are shelved can be closed at one end, with the opposite end opening into the local history collection reading room. Access should be limited. Rare materials, manuscripts, and archives require storage in secure, closed stack areas, locked bookcases, or locked rooms, with no self-service by patrons allowed. Manuscripts and archives are unique and cannot be replaced if lost or damaged.

Reference

The main objective of reference is to make the correct materials available to interested researchers. Reference procedures for local history collections are similar, regardless of where those collections are located.[6] Researchers range from knowing exactly what they wish to see when they arrive at the local history collection to just beginning a research project for which they have done little preparation. Reference questions range from the simplest directional questions about locating basic history texts to complex questions regarding economic development of the area. Finally, most local history collections serve researchers of all ages. Reference questions of all kinds are best answered by well-trained staff.[7]

If possible, the reference librarian or archivist should conduct a reference interview with each researcher embarking on a long-term project. The interview is especially helpful if the researcher is planning to use manuscripts and archives. The reference interview serves both the researcher and the archivist or librarian. The researcher has an opportunity to ask detailed questions about the collection; the materials in the collection; policies regarding photocopying, microfilming, and photography; and any special procedures required to use computers or typewriters in the reading room. When assisting a patron beginning long-term research, the librarian or archivist can often point out the materials most useful to the project and ask questions that give the researcher an opportunity to define the research topic. The reference interview can also give staff leads to other materials appropriate for the local history collection, for researchers may find materials related to their research in private hands and put the staff in contact with owners. Reference exit interviews can help staff determine what areas of reference need improvement, what services the researcher needed but did not receive, and what general complaints the researcher has about the service or the collection.

"The ability of the librarian to translate the query into terms that can be met by a given reference source is known as reference service," states William A. Katz in the standard library education reference textbook, *Introduction to Reference Services.*[8] Researchers may know what they are looking for but may not know how to ask for it. Because questions can be answered in a variety of ways, staff must learn to listen carefully and ask more questions if the researcher's queries are not clear. Researchers who ask for all materials on the United States Civil War are often looking for a specific piece of information, such as a map of the area of the battle in which an ancestor died. Pointing the patron to the Civil War subject entry in the card catalog is not enough. The staff member and the user must narrow the reference search to a more precise level. Reference staff must listen and analyze the questions in order to negotiate with the patron to reach the complete questions. Negotiating involves narrowing a broad question down to the actual need.[9]

Staffing patterns for the reference desk are very important. All staff who work in reference need full reference technique training. Researchers must not be made to rely on the memory of one archivist or one librarian. All reference staff can be trained to handle most reference questions. The best reference staff is one that rotates duties among technical and public services. The more staff members know about all the workings of the local history collection the better they can answer questions about the collection. Because memory varies from day to day and personal abilities may be negatively or positively affected by conditions in a staff member's life, reference desk rotation is beneficial to both staff and researchers. No one staff member is required to be "on" eight hours per day, and researchers receive an opportunity to interact with various members of the staff. However, certain staff may be called to the reference desk to answer questions in their area of expertise. For example, the state documents librarian should not be required to answer all document questions but should assist with complex questions requiring significant expertise. Of course, large local history collections may have an adequate number of reference staff to rotate reference desk duties, and small collections may have so few staff that all must be ready to do reference at all times. Staffing assignments must match the number of staff available.

In the best of all possible worlds, all information regarding the subjects in the local history collection would be in a computer database, and patrons could simply search for their topic online. But in the majority of local history collections, several different types of finding aids must be used to gain access to materials. Books, pamphlets, microfilm, serials, maps, and some audiovisual materials are accessible through a card catalog or a computer catalog. Other materials in manuscripts and archives, vertical files, special subject files, uncataloged materials, and photograph collections may be accessible through separate card catalogs, lists, in-house databases, inventories, and shelf lists. Therefore, the staff member should introduce each new patron to the finding aids and point out all steps necessary to locate materials. Patrons should be encouraged to ask questions. This lessens the frustration of the users and simplifies the staff's job, for patrons who receive thorough instructions on their first visit may not need repeated instructions on subsequent visits.

Can all print materials be found in the card catalog or the online catalog? How do subject files relate to manuscripts and archives inventories? How does the patron determine the proper location of an item? May bibliographies and inventories be photocopied for personal use? Is there a staff member who is familiar with the user's subject? Will the staff inform the user when new materials are received relating to his or her area of interest? Should the user visit other libraries for further information? The answers to these questions assist researchers in completing their work.

The archivist or librarian should stress to researchers that access to some archives materials takes time. Organizational archives are not created for researchers and their use. They are created as a result of the operation of the organization. Records of the local government exist as a result of the work of the government and are organized according to function. The main purpose of government archives is to "accomplish the legal purposes for which an agency has been created." Other values in the organizational archives are those that show evidence of the organization and functioning of the body that produced the records. "The information contained in government records is on persons, corporate bodies, things, problems, conditions, and the like with which the government body dealt."[10]

Ready reference collections of heavily used materials also facilitate patrons' work. Located on self-service shelves in the reading room, ready reference may include foreign language dictionaries, dictionaries, encyclopedias, guides to other local history collections, general histories of the area, bibliographies, city and organizational directories, guides to microfilm and other special collections, biographical files and dictionaries, atlases, and photographic histories. Patrons remove these items from the shelves for their use and return them to the reference desk for reshelving.

User surveys assist in understanding users needs and concerns. Questions to the users can cover reference, hours of operation, the scope of the collection, needs for photocopying equipment, funding, staffing, or any other subject that the staff feels would benefit the department and the users. The resulting information can assist in providing the administration with statistics to support longer or different hours, more staffing, or other needed services.

Gift items in the local history collection may have use restrictions other than their uniqueness. Donors sometimes request that manuscripts or archival materials they have given to the local history collection be restricted for a certain period of time. Restrictions exist because of the personal nature of items about people who are still living or simply because the donor wants to insure privacy for a limited time. In the deed of gift (see chapter 2 for a sample deed of gift), exact instructions regarding restrictions on the use of manuscripts and archival materials are listed. The local history collection has an obligation to make all materials available to researchers as soon as possible; therefore, collections with permanent restrictions should never be accepted by the department. What research value can a closed collection have, and how can the local history collection justify being a warehouse for the papers of one individual or group?

Other allowable restrictions protect items in poor condition. If an item is fragile, have it microfilmed or photocopied for researcher use and allow the original to be used only when a researcher must see it for bibliographic or handwriting validation. Microfilming fragile materials makes wider access to the materials possible through interlibrary loan programs and duplication of microfilm. Some items are restricted from photocopying or photographing. Photocopying will severely damage old and fragile materials. Photographing is less damaging if a flash is not used, but tightly bound items cannot be opened widely enough to be photographed. Items that are uncopyable should be clearly labeled as such. Researchers who need copies should be directed to other, less fragile and costly editions of the publication. Patrons should be encouraged to take notes from manuscripts and archives that cannot be copied. It is the responsibility of the local history collection staff to explain any restrictions to users and to assist in finding items that can be substituted for the restricted materials.

Copyright

The conflict between photocopying and copyright laws is an ever-present problem. The United States copyright law of 1976 states that anything copyrighted before 1906 is in the "public domain." Items in the public domain carry no restrictions on publishing or copying. Materials copyrighted after 1906 enter the public domain after 78 years. Complete copies of the copyright law (United States Code, Title 17) can be obtained from the Register of Copyrights, Library of Congress, Washington, DC 20559, and each local history collection should acquire one. Complete information on current copyright can be found in the law.

The copyright law allows "fair use" of copyrighted materials. Fair use permits limited copying of copyrighted works for use in a classroom, for a class paper or school project, or for research if such copies are not sold or given to library collections. Many manuscripts or archives groups received by the local history collection will contain photocopies of articles obtained for research use. Staff may retain these copies in the manuscripts or archives group, but other patrons using the materials must not copy them and must obtain permission to publish from the copyright holder. Permission to publish entire items that are copyrighted and already published must be obtained by the patron from the holder of the copyright. Limited quotation from copyrighted items is permissible under fair use. School children and college students may quote small portions from a copyrighted book for class projects and term papers. Genealogists may quote limited amounts in family histories. Graduate students may quote from copyrighted works in theses and dissertations. Copyright is a commercial commodity. Copyright holders have exclusive commercial rights to sell and profit from the publication of materials. When people publish extensively from copyrighted materials that belong to others, the owner of the copyright can lose money and a lawsuit may result. The local history collection staff are not police for copyrighted materials, but it is a courtesy to inform patrons of copyright restrictions. Signs regarding copyright must be placed on all photocopy machines (see fig. 6.1).

NOTICE

WARNING CONCERNING COPYRIGHT RESTRICTIONS

THE COPYRIGHT LAW OF THE UNITED STATES (TITLE 17, UNITED STATES CODE) GOVERNS THE MAKING OF PHOTOCOPIES OR OTHER REPRODUCTIONS OF COPYRIGHTED MATERIAL.

UNDER CERTAIN CONDITIONS SPECIFIED IN THE LAW, LIBRARIES AND ARCHIVES ARE AUTHORIZED TO FURNISH A PHOTOCOPY OR OTHER REPRODUCTION. ONE OF THESE SPECIFIED CONDITIONS IS THAT THE PHOTOCOPY OR REPRODUCTION IS NOT TO BE "USED FOR ANY PURPOSE OTHER THAN PRIVATE STUDY, SCHOLARSHIP, OR RESEARCH." IF A USER MAKES A REQUEST FOR, OR LATER USES, A PHOTOCOPY OR REPRODUCTION FOR PURPOSES IN EXCESS OF "FAIR USE," THAT USER MAY BE LIABLE FOR COPYRIGHT INFRINGEMENT.

THIS INSTITUTION RESERVES THE RIGHT TO REFUSE TO ACCEPT A COPYING ORDER IF, IN ITS JUDGMENT, FULFILLMENT OF THE ORDER WOULD INVOLVE VIOLATION OF COPYRIGHT LAW.

Fig. 6.1. Warning concerning copyright restrictions.

Current copyright laws cover unpublished materials as well. All works created after January 1, 1978, are automatically covered by United States copyright law without registration with the copyright office at the Library of Congress. Copyright exists for the creator of the work from the date of its creation until fifty years after the death of the author or creator if the item is never published. But the law passed in 1976 states that no copyright on unpublished materials shall expire before the year 2002. Therefore, a work written in 1900 whose author died in 1920 will not lose copyright until 2002. Copyright for works written in 2000 whose authors die in 2010 will expire in 2060. Manuscript and archive groups of nongovernmental records are copyrighted by their creators. Permission to publish from these works requires written permission from the creator, the copyright holder, or that person's descendants. When the local history collection files contain the names and addresses of copyright holders, this information should be given to patrons, if·requested. The patron is responsible for acquiring permission to publish.

Local, state, and federal government records do not fall under copyright laws and are in the public domain. Some government records, while not governed by copyright law, are restricted under the Privacy Act, which protects individuals from having items such as their school records made public. Local history collections holding government records need to be familiar with laws affecting the use of those records.

Requests to the local history collection for permission to publish items from the collection require careful handling. Reader registration rules give the procedures for writing the local history collection for permission to publish and the proper citation to use for quoting materials from the collection. (See chapter 3 for reader regulations.) The library may give permission to publish materials for which the copyright and literary rights have been given to the library by the original holders. However, the recipient of a letter cannot grant permission to use that letter, even if it has been included in his or her papers. Even if the library owns the original letter, the writer of the letter holds the copyright and is the only person who can transfer that copyright to the library.[11] In a 1987 case involving the letters written by novelist J. D. Salinger to others, the court ruled that the library holding the property (i.e., physical) rights to the letters could not give permission to publish those letters for they did not hold copyright; Salinger did. A similar court case involved the unpublished letters of L. Ron Hubbard. The court ruled that only the owners of the Hubbard copyright—the descendants or legal heirs—could give permission to publish; the library housing the letters could not.[12]

Special Services

Subject bibliographies of materials in the collection can reduce the research time needed by patrons and also reduce requests for staff assistance. Bibliographies prepared by staff, researchers, or volunteers may pertain to any subject covered by materials in the collection. Traditional bibliographies refer to printed materials, but in the local history collection, manuscript and archive groups receive entries in subject bibliographies as well. Subjects covered may include town history, genealogical materials, Civil War, theater materials, and a bibliography of ready reference materials. The Louisiana and Lower Mississippi Valley Collections has subject bibliographies on Spanish colonial materials in the collection, music-related materials, and Louisiana history materials both in the collection and in other libraries (see fig. 6.2, on pages 89-90). Small bibliographies may take only hours to prepare, while large ones, like a bibliography of Louisiana history, take several years. Bibliographies of a few pages can be photocopied for patrons visiting or writing the collection.

RESEARCH AID

Guides to manuscripts in the Louisiana and Lower Mississippi Valley Collections, Louisiana State University

(If a separate location is not shown the item is shelved on the LLMVC reference shelf in the Reading Room.)

Published:

Dean C. Allard, Martha L. Crawley, and Mary W. Edmison, *U.S. Naval History Sources in the United States* (Department of the Navy, Naval History Division, 1979). Z1249/N3/A48.

V. L. Bedsole, "Collections in the Department of Archives and Manuscripts, Louisiana State University," *Louisiana History* 1 (Fall 1960), 328-334. F366/L6238.

Henry Putney Beers, *French and Spanish Records of Louisiana: A Bibliographical Guide to Archive and Manuscript Sources* (National Archives and Records Administration, 1986). CD3047/B44.

Brian E. Coutts and Merna Whitley, "An Inventory of Sources in the Department of Archives and Manuscripts, Louisiana State University, for the History of Spanish Louisiana and West Florida," *Louisiana History*, XIX (Spring 1978), 213-249. F366/L6238.

Light Townsend Cummins and Glen Jeansonne, eds., *A Guide to the History of Louisiana* (Westport, Conn.: Greenwood Press, 1982). Z1289/G84.

Richard C. Davis, *North American Forest History: A Guide to Archives and Manuscripts in the United States and Canada* (Clio Books, 1977). Middleton Library Reference Z5991/D33.

Peter Duignan, *Handbook of American Resources for African Studies* (Hoover Institution, 1967). (Not available at LSU).

Thomas H. English, *Roads to Research* (University of Georgia Press, 1968). Z732/S92/E5.

Michele L. Fagan and Merna Whitley, "Britannica in Louisiana: An Annotated Inventory of Manuscript Sources Relating to Great Britain and the Empire in the Department of Archives and Manuscripts, Louisiana State University, Baton Rouge, Louisiana," (Baton Rouge: Subject Specialists Section of the Louisiana Library Association, 1982). (Ask at LLMVC Reference Desk or Z6621/L88/B747 Middleton Library).

Philip M. Hamer, ed., *A Guide to Archives and Manuscripts in the United States* (Yale University Press, 1961). CD3022/A45.

Andrea Hinding, ed., *Women's History Sources: A Guide to Archives and Manuscript Collections in the United States* (R. R. Bowker, 1979). Middleton Library Reference Z7964/U49/H56.

William R. Hogan, *Guide to Manuscript Collection in the Department of Archives, Louisiana State University* (Louisiana State University, 1940). CD3261/H5.

Fig. 6.2 continues on page 90.

Hubert Humphreys, *Louisiana Oral History Collections: A Directory* (Shreveport, LA: 1980).

Kathryn A. Jacob, ed., *A Guide to Research Collections of Former U.S. Senators, 1789-1982* (U.S. Senate Historical Office, 1983). CD3043/G85. (also BA/DOCS Y 1.1/31: Middleton Library)

Albert Krichmar, *The Women's Rights Movement in the United States, 1848-1970: A Bibliography and Sourcebook* (Scarecrow Press, 1972). (not available at LSU)

Cynthia P. Miller, ed., *A Guide to Research Collections of Former Members of the U.S. House of Representatives, 1789-1987* (Office for the Bicentennial of the U.S. House of Representatives, 1988). CD3043/G84. (also BA/DOCS Y 1.1/7:100-171: Middleton Library)

Ann Novotny, ed., *Picture Sources* (Special Libraries Association, 1975). Middleton Library N4000/S7.

J. Albert Robbins, ed., *American Literary Manuscripts: A Checklist of Holdings in Academic, Historical and Public Libraries, Museums, and Authors' Homes in the United States* (University of Georgia Press, 1977). Z6620/U5/M6.

Walter Schatz, ed., *Directory of Afro-American Resources* (R. R. Bowker, 1970). Middleton Library Reference Z1361/N39/R3.

T. Harry Williams and John Milton Price, "The Huey P. Long Papers at Louisiana State University," *Journal of Southern History* 36 (May 1970). F206/J68.

See Also: NUCMC, 1969-1985; and RLIN.

Unpublished:

Brian E. Coutts and Merna Whitley, "An Inventory of Sources for the History of Latin America in the Department of Archives and Manuscripts, Louisiana State University, Baton Rouge, Louisiana." (Ask at LLMVC reference desk.)

Merna Whitley, "Inventory of Oral History Materials in LLMVC." (Ask at LLMVC reference desk.)

Fig. 6.2. Research aid: Manuscripts. Reprinted with permission of the Louisiana and Lower Mississippi Valley Collections, LSU Libraries, Louisiana State University.

Additional services may include published and unpublished guides to the collection or subject guides to the collection. Guides contain concise descriptions of each group of materials or items listed and a subject and proper name index. Published guides are useful to researchers who need an overview of materials contained in the collection before traveling from other parts of the country to visit. Many libraries report their manuscript collections to the *National Union Catalog of Manuscript Collections* (NUCMC) at the Library of Congress. Using NUCMC, researchers throughout the country can learn what materials are available in local history collections.

Many patrons write to the local history collection before visiting in order to determine whether the collection contains materials necessary to their research. Responding to these inquiries consumes a great deal of staff time. If possible, patrons writing to the collection deserve quality assistance, just as those visiting the collection; however, on-site researchers should receive priority over those writing the repository. If reference letters cannot be answered within a reasonable time, prepare a form letter for response. The letter should explain why replies take a lengthy time and give an approximate date when an answer can be expected. Staff responsible for answering correspondence must adhere to time estimates. If the patron writes to the local history collection stating that he or she will be visiting and asks what materials are available on certain topics, send a form letter and brochure giving the hours of operation, location, general information on the collection, and the offer to assist the researcher on site. If the local history collection staff is so limited that it is impossible to answer reference letters, send the writer a form letter to that effect and suggest another library that may be able to help. Form letters that answer the collection's most frequently asked questions are time savers. A brochure is the most effective way to provide general information, telephone numbers, location, and hours of operation. Subject information sheets on holdings can contain general guides to beginning research in the local history collection.

For those local history collections that do attempt to answer reference letters, the investment in time is substantial. Staff responsible for answering letters must place time limits on letters that demand extensive research. These limits are dictated by the local history collection's staff size and use levels. The Louisiana and Lower Mississippi Valley Collections at Louisiana State University send patrons asking for extensive help by mail a list of private researchers who will contract to do research. The department does not guarantee the work of the contract researchers but simply provides a list of names.

Another service the local history collection can provide is a genealogical reference file. Patrons are encouraged to include their names, addresses, and the name of the families they are researching in the file, so that other researchers can contact them. Referrals aid researchers in other areas as well. The Louisiana and Lower Mississippi Valley Collections asks patrons to sign a card giving permission to the staff to inform other patrons of the area in which they are working, along with their name and address. Such information cannot be released unless the patron has given written permission.

Finally, local history collection staff may wish to assist patrons by doing online computer searches for them in national databases such as OCLC or RLIN or on online indexes to newspapers or periodicals. When extensive computer databases such as DIALOG and ERIC are searched, it is necessary to charge a fee to pay for the cost of the search. Indexes may be available on CD-ROMs, as well as in paper copies (*Wilsondisc*, *Books in Print Plus*). However, all patron services such as these require computer hookups or PCs capable of utilizing CD-ROMs. These capabilities exist in more and more libraries, enabling the local history collection to provide them to their patrons.

Libraries with in-house microfilming and photography departments offer excellent service to patrons requesting these services. Some local history collections have an ongoing program of microfilming manuscript and archive collections in order to protect the original materials and to provide wider service to researchers. Microfilms may be provided through interlibrary loan or sold to the patron. Patrons must understand that, even though they have purchased the microfilm of an item, the copyright is not transferred and they must still acquire permission to publish. The local history collection retains the negative microfilm at all times and provides positive copies for the use of patrons. It is important when microfilming manuscript or archive groups to microfilm entire groups or distinct series of the groups. Microfilming scattered correspondence from a manuscript group assists only one researcher. Microfilming all correspondence from a manuscript group assists many researchers and helps to preserve the originals. Title and target sheets on the microfilm indicate where the originals are located and who did the microfilming.

Photographing items from the collection also assists researchers and the collection. Of course, as with microfilming, patrons are required to pay the cost of making photographs (see fig. 6.3). Most libraries have limited photography facilities and may be able to make small black and white photographs but not color or extra large prints. Patrons most often request photographs of photographs, but may also ask for photographs of other materials. The local history collection should always retain the negative of the photograph, whether it is of a photograph or a handwritten letter from manuscript materials. Selling negatives enables a researcher to make numerous copies of the photograph, which violates fair use copyright. Copyright not owned by the local history collection belongs to the photographer. In the same way, photographs of children purchased by their parents are still the copyrighted property of the photographer. The parents own the physical property rights, but the person who made the photograph owns the creative copyright to the photograph. In some cases, the local history collection staff may want to allow patrons to photograph items in the collection themselves, especially if the collection has no photography services. If this is permitted, the patron should fill out a copy request form listing what has been photographed. Patrons should be informed of copyright and publishing restrictions, since these also apply to self-photographed items.

All items photocopied or photographed for patrons should be stamped with the name of the local history collection and library and should state that "reproduction is not permitted." Patrons should complete copy request forms for items that the collection will copy for them. These forms should state the price of the copies to the patrons (see fig. 6.4, on page 95). Photographs may take up to a week to be completed and photocopies several days. Patrons should be informed when they may pick up items. If they prefer to have copies mailed to them, they should be informed of any service charges involved. Patrons may feel that handling fees are excessive, but by the time a staff member makes the copies, fills out all the forms, prepares the invoices, and mails the items, considerable expense has been incurred. Patrons should be assured that they are only being asked to help reimburse such costs. Few libraries make a profit on any work they do for patrons.

ATLANTA HISTORY CENTER
PHOTOGRAPHIC REPRODUCTION AND PUBLICATION FEES
SEPTEMBER 1, 1992

PHOTOGRAPHIC REPRODUCTIONS of items in the collections are provided for specific, approved purposes only. Permission to publish requires prior written approval, use of the appropriate credit line, and advance payment of publication fees.

REPRODUCTION PRINTS of items in the collection; 8"x10" black-and-white glossy prints are standard. Print fee covers the price of photo reproduction of an existing negative for personal use only. If no transparency exists, the **Additional Fees** listed below will be added to this price. Any commercial or publication use of the image requires advance payment of the publication fees and permission to publish.

8"x10" print	$20.00	

Publication Fees:	Nonprofit	Commercial
One-time use, North American rights	$15.00	$30.00
One-time use, worldwide rights	$20.00	$40.00

RENTAL OF COLOR TRANSPARENCIES, 120 DAYS. 4"x5" transparencies are standard. Fee covers only the rental of existing transparencies of items in the collection for publication consideration and research. Publication of the images requires additional payment of the publication fees. If no transparency exists, the **Additional Fees** listed below will be added to this price. Transparency rental is subject to the conditions stated on the permission to publish form and advance payment of publication fees. Transparencies returned late will be subject to late charges.

Research or publication consideration	$ 20.00
Fee for lost/damaged transparency	$100.00

Publication Fees:	Nonprofit	Commercial
One-time use, North American rights	$35.00	$85.00
One-time use, worldwide rights	$45.00	$95.00

35mm PROJECTION SLIDES of items in the collections. New photography of museum objects requires curatorial approval; additional charges will apply. **Minimum order 5 slides.**

Lecture and classroom use	$ 4.00 per slide
Corporate presentation	$ 6.50 per slide
Publication consideration	$10.00 per slide

Publication Fees:	Nonprofit	Commercial
One-time use, North American rights	$35.00	$85.00
One-time use, worldwide rights	$45.00	$95.00

Fig. 6.3 continues on page 94.

ADDITIONAL FEES. If copy negatives or transparencies must be created to fill an order, additional charges apply. All negatives and transparencies created are the property of the Atlanta History Center and will be retained by the Center. New photography of museum objects requires curatorial approval; additional charges will apply.

Negatives from black-and-white originals smaller than 11"x14" $ 9.00
Negatives from black-and-white originals larger than 11"x14" $15.00
Transparencies from color originals smaller than 11"x14" $27.00
Transparencies from color originals larger than 11"x14" $35.00

If an original glass plate negative is used, there is a 50% surcharge on print price.

DELIVERY. Normal delivery time is **20 working days** from receipt of payment by first-class mail. Federal Express number required if order is to be shipped FedEx.

RUSH SERVICE (via FedEx or pick-up).
Ten working days from receipt of payment; add 50% additional to total costs.
Five working days from receipt of payment; add 100% additional to total costs.
Seventy-two hours from receipt of payment; add 200% additional to total costs.

3101 Andrews Drive, N.W. / Atlanta, Ga. 30305 / (404) 814-4000
Operated by the Atlanta Historical Society, Inc.

Fig. 6.3. Photographic reproduction and publication fees. Reprinted with permission of the Atlanta Historical Society, Atlanta, Georgia.

Not all local history collections or libraries can afford to have their own in-house photography laboratories. When the local history collection does not have this service, another means must be found to provide copies of photographs to patrons. A photographer in the community might contract with the library to provide photographic copying services. The contract should specify what services the photographer will provide to the local history collection, the prices of making copy photographs, the approximate time required to provide services, and a statement that the photographer will not retain negatives or copies of photographs belonging to the local history collection. Collection staff should deliver photographs to the photographer and be responsible for picking up orders and originals. A college or high school with a photography lab and photography students might also provide photographic services to the local history collection.

PHOTODUPLICATION REQUEST
LSU Special Collections
Hill Memorial Library

Library Use Only

Accepted _____
Approved _____
Est. Cost _____
Prepaid _____
Processed _____
Date _____

NAME _____

ADDRESS_____

_____

ID # _____

TELEPHONE _____

TYPE OF COPY
____ Electrostatic
____ Microprint
____ Microfilm
____ Photographs:
    No. of originals _____
    No. of copies each _____
    Size & Type _____

	No.	Ea.	Cost
Copies			
Microfilm			
Neg. Exp.			
Pos. Feet			
Reels &			
Cartons			
Photographs:			
Copy Neg.			
Prints			
Postage &			
Handling			
TOTAL COST			

COPY DELIVERY

_____ Will pick up copies, _____ Mail copies & invoice, _____ Charge account:_____

MATERIAL TO BE COPIED: (Give exact citation, call number, special instructions).

I agree to assume all responsibility for compliance with laws regarding copyright and literary right, and hold harmless Louisiana State University and Agricultural and Mechanical College, its agents, and employees from any lega action which may arise as a result of this transaction. I understand that charges are for services only, that photocopies remain the property of the Libraries of Louisiana State University and Agricultural and Mechanical College, and that they must be returned upon request.

_____   _____
       Signature   Date

Fig. 6.4. Photoduplication request form. Reprinted with permission of the Louisiana and Lower Mississippi Valley Collections, LSU Libraries, Louisiana State University.

Self-service photocopy machines aid researchers and reduce burdens on staff. If self-service copying is allowed, extra caution is required by staff and patrons. Each item to be copied must first be examined by staff. Government publications have no copyright restrictions; but if the item is so fragile that it will be destroyed by photocopying, it is the staff's responsibility to deny photocopying. All copyrights apply, whether items are photocopied by staff or by patrons. Some institutions allow self-service copying of manuscript and archive materials. Self-service photocopying of manuscript and archive items may be best for local history collections that have small numbers of researchers who can be more easily supervised and monitored. Collections with larger numbers of researchers may wish to have photocopying of manuscripts and archives done by staff. With this policy, manuscript removal forms are necessary to indicate not only what the patron wants copied but also indicate to staff where items are to be refiled (see fig. 6.5). After copying each item must be returned to its proper location within the folder or box from which it was taken. If a particular group of manuscripts or archives receives numerous photocopying requests, the staff should consider the group a candidate for microfilming; this will reduce the stress on the materials caused by photocopying. Other equipment the local history collection should provide is a self-service microfilm (or microfiche) reader/printer on which patrons can make their own copies of microfilmed materials.

Whatever type of library the local history collection is located within, users make the work of the collection worthwhile. Good patron service influences patrons to become future donors and established positive public relations in the community for the parent library.

MANUSCRIPT REMOVAL FORM

Patron's name _____
Date of removal _____
Name of collection _____
Collection location _____
Box # _____

Folder # _____

Date and/or description of item
(include number of leaves or
pages):

Proper acknowledgement of materials must
be made. The proper form of citation is the
full name of the collection used, followed by
"Louisiana and Lower Mississippi Valley
Collections, LSU Libraries, Louisiana State
University."

Permission to publish must be separately
requested.

For office use only:
Refiled
by _____ Date _____

Fig. 6.5. Manuscript removal form. Reprinted with permission of the Louisiana and Lower Mississippi Valley Collections, LSU Libraries, Louisiana State University.

Notes

1. The best source of concise information about local historical societies is the *Directory of Historical Agencies in North America*, 14th ed. (Nashville, TN: American Association for State and Local History, 1990).

2. George Chalou, "Reference," in *A Modern Archives Reader: Basic Readings on Archival Theory and Practice*, Maygene Daniels and Timothy Walch, eds. (Washington, DC: National Archives and Records Service, 1984), 261.

3. Society of American Archivists, "Standards for Access to Research Materials in Archival and Manuscripts Depositories," *American Archivist* 39 (1976): 411.

4. Gregor Trinkaus-Randall, "Preserving Special Collections Through Internal Security," *College and Research Libraries* 50 (1989): 449; see also Mary P. Wyly, "Special Collections Security: Problems, Trends, and Consciousness," *Library Trends* 36 (1987): 241-255.

5. Rare Books and Manuscripts Section Security Committee, "Guidelines for the Security of Rare Book Manuscripts and Other Special Collections," *College and Research Libraries News* 50 (1989): 397-401.

6. For an excellent discussion of reference work in archive and manuscript repositories, see Mary Jo Pugh, *Providing Reference Services for Archives and Manuscripts* (Chicago: Society of American Archivists, 1992), 1-123.

7. Karen F. Smith, "Robot at the Reference Desk?" *College and Research Libraries* 47 (1986): 487.

8. William A. Katz, *Introduction to Reference Services*, 5th ed. (New York: McGraw-Hill, 1987), 3.

9. John O. Christensen, et al., "An Evaluation of Reference Desk Service," *College and Research Libraries* 50 (1989): 470.

10. T. R. Schellenberg, "The Appraisal of Modern Public Records," in *A Modern Archives Reader*, Daniels and Walch, eds. 58.

11. For a thorough discussion of copyright and other legal matters, see Gary Peterson and Trudy H. Peterson, *Archives and the Law* (Chicago: Society of American Archivists, 1985).

12. "Justices Permit Strict Curbs on Use of Unpublished Writings," *Washington Post* (21 February 1990): 1, 4.

7 Public Relations and Outreach

Public relations and outreach programs take many forms and serve several purposes, including education. The main purpose is to increase public awareness about the local history collection and thereby increase use. Press releases, newsletters, publications, exhibitions, and presentations by local history collection staff reach more potential users than word of mouth alone.

Even local history collections with small budgets should seek to provide educational experiences for their users. The most important aspect of this educational mission is to make materials available to patrons. Public relations and outreach programs assist in acquiring new users of, and donors to, the local history collection. Many potential users are also potential donors, and satisfied users are an effective public relations tool. More users and more donors can translate into more support from the parent institution.

Outreach and public relations are alike in many ways, but they are essentially different. The ultimate goal of public relations programs and outreach or educational programs is the same—to inform the public about the work of the local history collection. How then do they differ? Public relations can be defined as "the business of fostering public goodwill toward the institution," and is essentially an administrative function of information dissemination. Outreach is the education program or action taken to create something which publicity, that is public relations, can be about. Outreach, or user education as it applies to archives, is "the education and training of actual and potential users of archival materials in matters such as reference service; the availability, use, and interpretation of archival materials; and the value of archival work."[1] When "local history collection" is substituted for "archives" in the above statement, the definition still applies.

A local history collection does not need an elaborate array of public education programs in order to reach its public. A simple plan can be sufficient to the needs of a small, minimally staffed collection. A public relations program can include newsletters, press releases, newspaper articles, journals, brochures, and public appearances by the local history collection staff. Proper planning and execution will mean success.

Public Relations

Public relations programs should relate to the mission, collecting policies, and objectives of the local history collection. Public relations and outreach programs focusing on subjects outside the purview of the collecting policies are more detrimental than helpful. Priorities and resources should be evaluated as the first step in the program. A local history collection staffed by one or two people and assisted by volunteers has few resources available to allocate to public relations. Small collections can plan to incorporate their public relations activities with those of the parent library or institution. Public relations activities can be divided into two segments: publicity relating to the basic functions of the collection such as acquisitions, announcements of new finding aids, and personnel and volunteer activities; and publicity relating to outreach functions such as exhibits, lectures, and classes. A yearly planning worksheet assists staff. The yearly planning sheet for public relations lists types of publicity, staff member responsible for preparing press releases, number of such activities per year, percent of staff time required to perform each activity, and if possible, where time will be taken from, that is, reference desk time or processing time of staff members (see fig. 7.1). Staff time is a resource just like money in the budget; only 100% of it can be spent. BEGIN SMALL. Overly ambitious public relations or outreach programs are likely to fail, and such failure will be demoralizing to the local history collection staff, volunteers, and public.

In their manual for public programs, Ann E. Pederson and Gail Farr Casterline suggest an "add-on approach," or a "pattern for coordinated program development through several levels, or phases, of complexity."[2] Simply put, the "add-on approach" is designed to do just that, add on to what has been done before. Once a program such as press releases about new acquisitions is in place, then more projects can be built on the procedures already established. A second public relations project might be a weekly or monthly column written by local history collection staff and published in the local newspaper, the campus newspaper, the company newsletter, or other appropriate media. By using the contact persons established for the press releases, the local history collection can determine who is willing to publish such a column. Guidelines for news columns and the appropriate contacts and deadlines should be added to the handbook for press releases. The handbook should also include a record of which staff are responsible for press releases and news columns. All staff may participate in all projects, but definite responsibilities for public relations should be assigned each year. If the responsible staff member wishes to delegate his or her assignments to another staff member for a particular project, all staff need to be informed of the reassignment (see fig. 7.2, on page 102).

If there is a staff member who is a particularly talented writer or editor, that person can serve as the "staff editor." The staff editor reviews all materials written by department staff that will be sent out to the public, including press releases, brochures, newsletters, and other publicity about outreach events.

LOCAL HISTORY COLLECTION PUBLIC RELATIONS PLAN

Activity	Actors	Responsibilities	Number per Year	Percent of Staff Time	Cost
1. News releases on new acquisitions	news release coordinator	edit & issue	quarterly	2 percent	staff time postage
	acquisitions staff	write news releases		2 percent	
	secretarial	typing & mailing		1 percent	
2. Informational brochure	department head	write copy	one every five years	2 percent	staff time
	staff editor	edit copy, take to printer		1 percent	designer & printer costs cost of
	secretarial	typing		1 percent	paper and photography
3. Public appearances	department head	write & present speeches	5 per quarter	5 percent	staff time time away
	other staff as appropriate	write & present speeches		2 percent	from local history
	secretarial	typing & schedule appointments		2 percent	collection

Fig. 7.1. Local history collection public relations plan.

Press Releases

Press releases about the daily activities of the collection are an excellent means of publicity, and if planned correctly, require a minimum of staff time. Each month's acquisitions can be announced to the public through a press release to the local newspapers, campus newspaper, alumni newsletter, library newsletter, professional library journals, professional association journals, and organizational newsletters. As with any newspaper article, the press release should include who, what, when, where, and why. When manuscripts and archives are accessioned, a brief description of the new acquisition can be prepared by the staff member who accessions the materials, and staff members responsible for checking in the new books can prepare a list. Do not attempt to publish a monthly listing of all books received or items added to the vertical file in the local media. Instead, prepare a quarterly press release of significant new books in the collection to give to patrons. Send the list to the local news media, who may find occasion to use excerpts from the list as filler. Extremely unusual gifts or purchases of rare books warrant a press release, as do manuscript or archive acquisitions. Check with donors to determine if they wish to have their names mentioned in such press releases. Giving publicity to a donor who does not with it can be bad public relations.

Archival function	Phase I: The Personal Approach	Phase II: The Group Approach	Phase III: The Community Approach
Reference Services	Signs Simple chart of reference room	Mini-seminars for beginning researchers Slide-tape show	Regular workshops on archival research, focusing on popular topics and frequently asked questions Workshops for clients of different ages and levels of experience
Finding aids	Brochure describing institution's purpose, holdings, facilities and terms of use	Pamphlet guide to holdings	Comprehensive inventory coupled with specialized subject groups
Access	Invitations to potential clients (individuals and groups) to use archives	Loans to research institutions	Microfilm publications
Appraisal/ Acquisition	Personal contacts to donors and depositing agencies, using basic brochure Slide talks for civic service and educational groups	Feature articles and news releases on major holdings and new acquisitions Workshop on identifying materials of historical value Brochure on making donations to the collections	Documentation projects
Preservation	Speech with slides showing types of damage and items that have been conserved	Workshops and demonstrations of proper conservation techniques, e.g., "Caring for Family Documents and Photographs"	Slide-tape presentation distributed to fellow archivists
Arrangement and Description	Leaflet explaining how materials are made available to researchers	Volunteer program for archival processing	Institute on archival techniques for fellow professionals
Education and Research	Tour of the archives Speech about archives illustrated with slides Occasional newspaper articles about significant items in the collection	Lectures based on research projects undertaken at the archives, given by staff or invited speakers	Major exhibits and publications Arrangements for producing television and radio programs based on subjects documented in the collections Full range of conferences and workshops on various aspects of historical and archival work

Fig. 7.2. The add-on approach for program development. From Ann E. Pederson and Gail Farr Casterline, *Archives and Manuscripts: Public Programs* (Chicago: Society of American Archivists, 1982), 14. Reprinted with permission of the Society of American Archivists.

Some libraries have public relations departments that review all press releases and prepare them for final distribution. Libraries within museums, universities and colleges, and businesses may have access to a well-defined public relations department and should utilize this service. Even when the collection's parent institution has a public relations department, press releases will require some time from the local history collection staff, and this requires planning. It is always helpful to have a handbook to show the proper format for local history collection press releases; the names, addresses, and phone numbers of contact persons for each agency to which press releases are sent; and the deadlines of the publications in which local history collection press releases need to appear. These types of press releases will take the least amount of time of any public relations activity and will place the name of the local history collection before the public.

Brochures

Another simple and direct form of public relations is a brochure about the local history collection that can be given to researchers, visitors, people attending public programs, and handed out by staff at functions they attend. The best brochures are simple and to the point and describe the local history collection in direct terms, list the services, and give a brief summary of items accepted for gifts.

Brochures can be created expensively or inexpensively. Basic colors are most acceptable, and one-color with no color separation is the most inexpensive type of printing. Illustrations are desirable, and the local history collection's or the parent library's logo adds extra interest. Desktop publishing packages for personal computers (e.g., PageMaker by Aldus, Ventura Publisher by Xerox, ReadySetGo by Manhattan Graphics, and KeyPublisher from Global Computer Supplies) have made brochure and newsletter production a cost-effective public relations tool for many institutions. Brochures created from camera-ready copy taken to the printer is much less expensive than brochures needing layout and design. Graphic design students from local colleges, trade schools, and high schools may be helpful in brochure production. If the parent library has a brochure, the local history collection brochure can be designed in a similar style and color scheme. Matching brochures fix the relationship between the parent library and the local history collection in the public mind. Colleagues can give helpful information and samples of brochures they have prepared.

Newsletters

Many libraries publish a monthly, quarterly, or occasional newsletter that is mailed to patrons, donors, board members, faculty members, colleagues, and friends groups. Newsletters can be inexpensive or very costly, depending upon their purpose, clientele, and money allocated to production. Who is the newsletter's clientele? The parent library's newsletter, directed to all persons holding public library cards, is the appropriate place for the local history collection to include its press releases on acquisitions and other news columns. Use of an established medium minimizes the work of staff. Likewise, newsletters directed to friends groups or other special interest groups will be an appropriate place for press releases and news columns, with an occasional feature article about the work of the local history collection. Such special interest newsletters devote most of their space to the activities of the special interest group. However, if the friends group is devoted solely to the local history collection, the more news about the collection the better. Newsletters lose their effectiveness if they are not timely. Reporting on events that are to happen in the future and then delaying publication of the newsletter until after the event places the local history collection in a bad light to patrons. Maintain a mailing list of those who ask to receive the newsletter. Print extra copies of the newsletter to have available in the library and local history collection.

If the local history collection is to publish its own newsletter devoted solely to its work and activities, it is critical to allocate staff and budget to the task. This often means that staff are drawn from other functions. Evaluation of staff resources is imperative to the successful production of newsletters. Decisions should be made regarding the number of times each year the newsletter will be published; the size and format of the newsletter; whether it will be produced by desktop publishing, a design and layout professional, or some other method; who the printer will be; approximate cost for printing; type of paper to be used and how it is to be folded for mailing; and how the newsletter is to be disseminated. This information should be incorporated into the public relations handbook, as well as the names of staff and any volunteers who are responsible for newsletter production.[3]

Whatever the mode of production, most newsletters are distributed by mail. Such a procedure requires a mailing list and a method for keeping it current. A staff person must be responsible for the maintenance of the mailing list. The staff member may utilize clerical staff, volunteers, or students to assist with this work when they are available. Procedures regarding the mailing list and post office requirements should be included in the public relations manual. Software packages designed to handle mailing lists are available for most personal computers and word processors. Manual systems are still acceptable for small lists and small local history collections. Whatever system is used, only an up-to-date mailing list is cost-effective. Most organizations begin mailing lists with the most readily available names and addresses: donors, researchers who have completed registration forms, friends groups, news media, appropriate professional organizations, and colleagues. In the first newsletter, ask those receiving it to pass it on to others who might be interested and ask recipients to send in their names and addresses if they wish to be placed on the mailing list. Stamp or print "address correction requested" on the newsletter itself. Then the post office will notify the library if the address is incorrect. Also hand out copies of the newsletter to patrons using the local history collection and add them to the mailing list if they wish. After responses are received from the first newsletter, update the mailing list before sending out the next one. Remove names of those who indicate that they do not wish to receive the newsletter; add those who have requested to be added; make changes to addresses with "address corrections" from the post office; and delete the names of those on newsletters returned as undeliverable by the post office. Some newsletters should be saved to mail to people requesting them after the first mailing has gone out.

Post office requirements regarding "bulk mailing" cost vary from year to year, so it is best to talk to a representative of the post office about the most effective and least expensive way to mail newsletters or other items from the local history collection. Bulk mail requires proof of nonprofit status of the institution to qualify for the least expensive mailing. The parent library of the local history collection may already have such a designation and can produce the necessary bulk mail number.

Journals

An even more ambitious public relations and outreach activity is publishing a journal on a regular or occasional basis. A journal seeks to educate its readers and may be defined as a series of articles devoted to a subject, place, or time period. Most familiar journals are those received from professional associations. Many local history collections, however, do publish journals. The publication of a journal that includes lengthy articles by scholars and other interested writers involves time, expense, and effort. A working relationship with a professional printer is mandatory, and an experienced editor is a necessity. Before beginning a journal, carefully review the need for such a publication. Is there a similar journal already being published? Will the market and subject matter support two local history journals? It is unlikely that any organization could publish a journal and distribute it for free. If it is determined that there is sufficient interest in the journal, staff resources should then be assessed. Is there a staff member or volunteer who is an experienced editor with time to devote to production of a journal? Is clerical staff available? Who will pay for the journal? Even if the subscriptions cover the costs, it will take time to build the necessary cash reserves to pay for production. Someone will have to bear the cost of the first issue. How will subscribers be attracted?

Establish a review procedure. Will there be an editorial board who review the articles? Will there be a blind review process whereby contributors do not know who reviews their articles, or some other method? Editors should not bear the entire burden of accepting or rejecting articles. This is a task that requires assistance. Acceptance criteria must be established and published in the journal for potential authors. The editor must be honest and timely with authors, for they, too, are donors, patrons, and friends of the local history collection.

If these questions are answered positively and plans to publish a journal are accepted by the administration, the local history collection should begin to solicit articles for inclusion in the first issue and to develop a list of potential authors. Ask for submission of articles in the newsletter, place notices in other journals soliciting articles, and request articles verbally from patrons, donors, and other appropriate persons. Establish a review procedure. Get advise from colleagues who run publishing programs. Occasional pamphlets and catalogs of the collections may be the most valuable publishing venture for medium-sized, moderately funded local history collections. As many university presses will agree, publishing programs are seldom profitable. Local history collections should enter cautiously into publishing ventures. The benefits of a publishing program, especially a local history journal, can be measured in terms of heightened community involvement with the local history collection.

Brochures, newsletters, press releases, news columns, and journals are all public relations media and serve as outreach activities as well. Outreach, education programs, and public programs are used interchangeably by the local history collection to reach out to the public and provide broader services. Outreach programs may include exhibitions, lectures and symposia, classes, fellowships for visiting scholars, friends groups, oral history projects, media productions, and publishing programs. Creating an idea file to which all staff members add their ideas for publicity and outreach programs, including exhibitions, is a great way to generate ideas.

Outreach Programs

Exhibitions

Large and small local history collections tend to produce exhibitions. The Smithsonian Institution in Washington, D.C., is the national local history collection that produces major exhibitions for the American public. The Smithsonian expends millions of dollars per year for this purpose, but those exhibitions are no more important than the small scale exhibitions mounted by the Louisiana and Lower Mississippi Valley Collections or any other local history collection.

How-to manuals on exhibitions are available from the American Association for State and Local History, the American Association of Museums, the Society of American Archivists, and others. Several simple rules apply, however, for exhibitions of local history materials. Security and temperature and humidity control are just as important in the exhibition area and cases as they are in the local history collection reading room and stacks. Perhaps they are even more important in the exhibition area. Cases being used to exhibit local history collection materials must have locks that are unbreakable or trigger alarms when tampered with. Exhibitions tend to highlight valuable or unusual materials from the collection, not only to the desired visitors but to visiting thieves as well. Exhibitions held in areas outside the local history collection staff's viewing area require monitoring by security staff or other library staff for the entire period the exhibit is open to the public. If possible, have visitors to the exhibit wear visitors badges and sign in and out. If this is not possible, be certain the exhibit area is in the direct and obvious view of staff members at an information or reference desk. Never, for any reason, exhibit books, photographs, or manuscripts that are small enough to be hidden in clothing outside a locked case. If photographs or manuscripts are to be displayed on a wall, use copies or facsimiles or frame them in large bulky frames or mats. All staff should be alerted to be especially cautious about items on exhibition.

In addition to security, temperature and humidity control is a critical problem for exhibition staff. This problem is too often overlooked by local history collections in preparing exhibitions. In order for the materials to be properly viewed, lights are usually needed in cases. Such lights increase the interior temperature of the exhibit cases to a level undesirable for the preservation of library materials. Also, as the temperature rises in the exhibit case, the humidity goes down. At night when the lights are turned off, temperatures will decrease and humidity may rise. Papers affected by such temperature and humidity changes will lose flexibility and strength. Therefore, if lighting systems that create minimal temperature and humidity changes are not available, a practical solution may be to turn on the lights in the exhibit cases only when visitors are present. The library conservation unit at BookLab, Inc., recommends that "at minimum the cases should be provided with a passive capacity to buffer humidity change, should seal tightly and have no air exchange ventilation. The glazing should have a filtering capacity to screen ultraviolet rays, and the case illumination should be provided by exterior lighting only."[4]

Once security and environmental concerns are addressed, then the shape, size, theme, and purpose will vary from exhibition to exhibition. Providing exhibitions for the public has become a tradition for most local history collections with the mistaken impression that exhibitions are easy and cheap to produce. This is not the case, however, and in planning public programs local history collections need to evaluate carefully the return on the investment. Background research and label writing take enormous amounts of time to do properly. Planning is imperative. Who will be responsible for the exhibition? Who will be the curator? Will the exhibition program be on a continuing basis with exhibitions occurring year round, or will exhibitions be occasional activities that take place only in conjunction with special events such as commemorative celebrations, lectures, or workshops?

For a small local history collection with limited staff, one theme, semi-permanent exhibitions are an excellent outreach tool. Such exhibitions should be mounted for from six months to a year using reproductions of photographs and documents made just for the exhibition. Other objects, such as books, should be rotated every three months at the maximum. Such semi-permanent exhibitions limit the number of staff hours needed to maintain schedules. Another solution is to borrow traveling exhibitions from state museums and national organizations, such as the Smithsonian. Even these will require work by the staff and some financial investment. There will often be a borrowing fee; and the borrowing institution is responsible for shipping the exhibition to its next destination. Such costs should be planned for in the exhibition budget.

Instead of full scale exhibitions, small local history collections should consider appropriate displays that simply place items on view. Exhibitions should interpret, tell a story, and educate. Displays only present items with minimal labels, but they still have educational value. Whatever the size or scope of the exhibitions, programming exhibits for the local history collection requires significant use of staff time. Few local history collections will have a staff member devoted solely to exhibitions or outreach; therefore, staff time comes from other functions. One staff member assigned overall responsibility for exhibition scheduling each year plans for staff assignments to the exhibition program.

To publicize exhibitions, procedures already in place for producing press releases and newsletters should be utilized. Staff assigned such duties work with exhibition staff to gather materials for press releases and newsletter information. Publicity about exhibitions is important to their success. Although there will be a ready-made group of viewers for the exhibition from among regular patrons of the local history collection, new patrons can be attracted to the collection through exhibitions. Publicity about an exhibition may draw visitors who have never used the local history collection, which is one of the main goals of outreach programs. Exhibitions, of course, complement lecture programs, classes held in the local history collection, or publications drawn from the materials of the local history collection. A procedures handbook should be developed for the exhibition program, whatever its size, and should be used when making yearly plans. Planning and flexibility are the keys to effective exhibition programs, large or small.

Evaluation of exhibitions, as well as other outreach activities, assist improved planning and production of future outreach activities. Staff review of the following questions is very useful:

1. Did the exhibition meet the goals set by the local history collection?

2. Was the response of those visiting the exhibition positive?

3. What was the total cost in money and staff time?

4. What areas can be improved?

5. Was there sufficient publicity for the exhibition (or outreach program)?

6. Would the local history collection present the exhibition (or program) again?

7. Did the benefits to the local history collection outweigh the costs?

Questionnaires should be developed to solicit responses from the public visiting the exhibition or attending the outreach program. Brief, clear, positively phrased questions are best (see fig. 7.3). Questionnaires should be answered at the end of the program or the visit because people seldom return evaluation questionnaires through the mail. If possible, make the questionnaire a verbal one administered by staff at the end of the program.

PROGRAM VISITOR QUESTIONNAIRE

Name (Optional):

Address (Optional):

Program attended:

1. How were you informed of the dates and times for the program you attended?

_____ newspaper _____ invitation _____ agency newsletter _____ friend
_____ other (please specify):

2. Why was this program of interest to you?

_____ school related _____ research related _____ personal interest
_____ curiosity _____ brought my family _____ other (please specify):

3. Did the program meet your expectations?

Your overall rating of this conference is:

_____ poor _____ fair _____ uncertain _____ good _____ very good

4. Would you attend future programs on this topic?

5. Do you wish to be included on our mailing list? If so, please include name and address at the top of this form.

6. Please give us your suggestions for future programs.

Thank you for attending the programs of the Somewhere Public Library.
Please leave this form at the desk near the exit. Your comments are appreciated.

Fig. 7.3. Program visitor questionnaire.

Evaluations kept in the program or exhibition file help future planners of local history collection programs. Each exhibition's or program's file should contain all materials relating to the planning and execution of the program. Exhibition labels, checklists, loan forms, correspondence, budgets, bills and receipts, staff assignment sheets, and a report by the supervising staff member are required parts of the file. Good record keeping for the local history collection prevents staff from recreating plans or making similar errors in future plans.

Lectures

A natural extension of the exhibition program is the lecture series. Guest speakers invited to open an exhibition or to give a speech highlighting some aspect of a local history collection exhibit are popular outreach activities. If the library already has an ongoing lecture series, the local history collection can request that one or two slots each year be dedicated to local history themes. Or the collection may serve as a catalyst for the development of a new ongoing lecture series. Outside funding for lectures can sometimes be obtained from grant agencies. Another potential source of lecture assistance can come from a cooperative program with local community colleges, universities, or high schools. Teachers can require attendance at the local history collection lecture series and can serve as speakers. As with any other outreach program, planning and effective use of staff resources are the keys to a successful lecture program. What is the lecture series intended to achieve? Who on the staff will be responsible for overseeing the lecture series? Publicity about the lecture series or guest speakers can be handled by the staff assigned to prepare press releases.

An elaboration of the lectureship series is a concentrated one-to-two day symposium on a subject featured by the local history collection. A symposium consists of several speakers presenting formal papers and then leading discussion groups regarding their subjects. Symposia may be sponsored by the local history collection, the friends organization, or a department of the local college or university. Publicity is critical for the success of the lecture series or symposia, just as it is for the exhibition program.

Friends Groups and Volunteers

Many patrons of local history collections enjoy attending lecture series and opening of exhibitions that also include receptions. Receptions involve serving food and drink and can be costly and time consuming. While it is best not to involve staff resources in presenting receptions, friends of the library groups may be an appropriate resource for such activities. Friends groups serve many other valuable purposes as well. The Friends of the Library of the Louisiana State University Libraries hold an annual book bazaar that has raised as much as $50,000 per year, which is donated to the library. While not every friends organizations may be expected to be that successful, they can still be a source of additional funds, acquisitions, volunteer staff, new patrons, and other assistance.

Developing a friends of the local history collection will, in the beginning, require allocation of staff time to locate a group of interested community members to serve as the first steering committee. Some of the same community supporters who have served on documentation strategy committees, lectureship programs, and other special events may be solicited to serve. Staff serve only as ex-officio members. The American Library Association has provided guidelines for friends organizations.[5] The main purpose of the friends organization is to promote the activities and needs of the local history collection to the community. Friends groups sponsor lecture series, exhibitions, publications, newsletters, workshops, and research fellowships. They also serve as fund-raising organizations for local history collections through book sales, publications, endowment funds, and solicitation of grants. They work in conjunction with the staff of the local history collection and the parent library administration to ensure that their activities correspond with the institution's mission and goals. Friends groups usually have a membership fee that funds their activities. The friends membership list can be included on mailing lists for newsletters, invitations, and other mailings.

Members of friends organizations may also be the source for volunteers. Volunteer programs have provided exceptional workers for local history collections, developed positive public relations with the community, and been the source for valuable acquisitions. However, effective volunteer programs are not free, they require planning and proper administration. As with all outreach activities, volunteer programs demand an investment of staff time. One staff member should be assigned to be the coordinator of the volunteer program and prepare a procedures manual. Volunteers are asked to sign a simple contract form indicating the hours they will volunteer, the type of work they will be assigned, their home address and telephone number, and the name of the person to contact in an emergency (see fig. 7.4, on page 112). The local history collection volunteer coordinator also signs the form and provides a copy to the volunteer. A file is kept on each volunteer. The library administration should be consulted regarding any insurance restrictions for volunteer workers. Badges are needed that identify volunteers from other staff. Volunteers should not be made to feel that they are not trusted, but do not give volunteers tasks that require them to be in the stacks or working with archives and manuscripts or rare books unsupervised.

Welcome as a volunteer worker to the Louisiana and Lower Mississippi Valley Collection, Special Collections, Louisiana State University Libraries. The LLMVC is a specialized collection of books, microforms, maps, and manuscripts covering the culture and history of the Mississippi Valley and Louisiana for all periods. As such it represents a significant research collection for patrons from the University, other universities and the public. We attempt to make materials received in the LLMVC available to such researchers as efficiently and effectively as possible while also maintaining the highest preservation standards.

You as a volunteer can help us to achieve such goals. We ask therefore that you read and agree to abide by the following:

Volunteer work periods should be a minimum of three consecutive hours.

Volunteer will provide a schedule of their work times to the staff member supervising their work. The staff member will provide such schedules to the Head of LLMVC. When schedules must be changed or cannot be met the volunteer will notify the supervising staff member.

Volunteers will follow all security, safety, and work procedures of the Special Collections Library.

Signature _____ Date _____

Assigned to: _____
                    (staff member's name and name of project)

Schedule:

Fig. 7.4. Volunteer employment form. Reprinted with permission of the Louisiana and Lower Mississippi Valley Collections, LSU Libraries, Louisiana State University.

The coordinator of the volunteer program should begin by determining what types of projects can be done by volunteers. Volunteers wish to contribute to an organization that truly needs their help. Both the local history collection and the volunteer must benefit by the program. It is more effective for the volunteer and the local history collection if volunteers work closely with collection staff at all times. The balance between supervised work and work that is meaningful is difficult to achieve. Some examples that have been successful for local history collections are: vertical file maintenance projects, clipping of news stories from newspapers and filing and indexing; indexing local newspapers; information desk assistance; telephone answering; gathering information from donors of photographs; rehousing photographs into archival sleeves and folders; oral history interviewing and assistance with maintenance of a genealogical reference collection. When volunteers arrive, they should be matched to the tasks available and interviewed by the staff member who will supervise them. Colleagues are a source of ideas on successful volunteer projects and of information about administration of a volunteer program. Volunteer projects should be listed in the local history collection or friends newsletter to solicit volunteers. Happy volunteers will speak to their friends about becoming volunteers for the local history collection and thereby increase the number of available, qualified volunteers.

Varied Projects

Outreach may involve bringing outside scholars into the local history collection or taking the local history collection out into the community or both. Ways to bring the public to the library include classes and workshops. Staff should discuss with patrons, donors, volunteers, and friends group members what type of classes and programs would be useful to the community. Classes on how to use the local history collection, research genealogies, preserve family photographs and papers, donate family papers and organizational records to the local history collection, research using local newspapers, or write local or family history are just a few examples of classes the local history collection could sponsor and teach. Workshops may last several hours or a day focusing on one topic with one or more speakers. Workshops usually give the attendees some demonstrations or hands-on experiences.

Research fellowships are an excellent project for a friends organization to fund. The Newberry Library, the American Antiquarian Society, the Congressional Research Center at the University of Oklahoma, and many others provide limited one-to-three month fellowships for scholars to visit the collection and do research. The scholars receive a stipend (a small financial grant) while visiting the collection. Many of these fellowships are very competitive and prestigious. The benefits to the local history collection are more published materials written from the collections, visibility in the scholarly community, prestige for the community, educational interchanges for the staff and scholars, possible sources for acquisitions, and stimulation for fund-raising. Again, such a program requires allocation of staff resources and planning. A fellowship committee must be appointed to select the fellows; application forms and procedures devised; appropriate housing located, even if the scholars are responsible for their own accommodations; and other details managed, all of which require large amounts of time.

In addition to bringing people to the local history collections, outreach programs can involve taking the local history collection to the community. Talks by staff to local and regional organizations can showcase the local history collection and its work. Different staff members may be asked to speak to community organizations. Invitations may come frequently, or infrequently, after the community is aware that staff members are available for such talks. Invitations must be balanced with other staff responsibilities and commitments. Most organizations are flexible in their speakers' scheduling. More elaborate projects involve slide/tape programs that are about the local history collection and its work, or that are based on subjects in the local history collection. A promotional slide show could include slides of the facilities, slides of materials collected, and slides of staff members and volunteers working. For example, the story of a local business or church or the life of early women settlers could be the subject of such a program using photographs, newspapers, letters, diaries, and organizational records in the local history collection. Subject-oriented programs provide a wider knowledge of local history for the community and help to solicit acquisitions. State humanities councils (such as the Louisiana Endowment for the Humanities) are state branches of the National Endowment for the Humanities (NEH) and provide grant funds for educational programs directed to adult audiences, including lectures. Slide/tape or video programs developed with grants become permanent outreach programs. Other slide/tape or video programs may be developed by students from high school honor classes, college history students, or graduate students in many different fields.

Preparation of slide/tape or video programs takes much more staff time than public speaking engagements. Before a slide program or video program can be produced, many hours are devoted to research, script preparation, and selection of images and photography. Production companies can be hired to produce programs, but they are expensive and will require staff involvement. What are the benefits the local history collection hopes to derive from a media production? Will the benefits outweigh the cost of production? Is it a product that can be used for many years? It is a simple mechanical program that does not require multiple machines and trained media operators? Who will be responsible for scheduling such programs for community organizations? Once a media program is produced and available for use, the program should be advertised in the local history collection newsletter, friends newsletter, and press releases. A contact person's address and phone number should be listed.

Oral history, recognized as a way to supplement written records, is another outreach program that benefits the community and the local history collection. Famous and ordinary people are formally interviewed by historians, archivists, librarians, and volunteers in order to gain their view of the world and events as they saw them. Oral history can be a valuable addition to the local history collection.

Oral history requires careful planning, training, and administration. Staff should consult oral history manuals, oral history technical leaflets from the American Association for State and Local History, and publications from the Oral History Association.[6] Someone who has been involved with oral history programs in another local history collection could serve as a consultant to the planning stages of the program. Who are the interviewers? Who are the interviewees, and why do these people deserve being interviewed for the local history collection? Volunteers can be used as interviewers after receiving careful training on how to prepare for the interview, how to use the equipment, and the necessity of preparing proper forms. Oral history interviewing requires preparation on the part of the interviewer by researching the local history collection for information about the life and times of the person to be interviewed. Oral histories can focus on a person's entire life or on just one period or aspect, such as their political career. Whatever the focus, the interviewer should formulate questions in advance and be responsible for keeping the interviewee on track in a diplomatic way. The interview may take one hour or several hours. The interviewer and the interviewee should be prepared to continue the interview through several appointments if necessary.

Once the interview is completed, the tape should be transcribed. This requires a typist to listen to the tape, type what is heard, and present the typed version to the interviewer to review. Corrections may need to be made in names, some dates, and unclear words, but actual editing except for punctuation is limited. Transcripts should then be forwarded to the interviewee for editing. Interviewees should be asked to do minimal editing and return the transcript with signed donor forms (see fig. 7.5, on page 116). The tapes and the transcripts are accessioned in the local history collection and handled as archival materials for cataloging and research.

Oral history programs require time, planning, and dedication by the local history collection staff. Volunteers make oral history programs possible in many cases, but local history collection staff must administer the program.

Review

Public relations professionals recommend a "public relations audit" for assessing the organization's visibility in the community and among colleagues. The audit attempts to answer several important questions: How does the local history collection's audience(s) perceive it? Does that perception match the local history collection's desired image? Are the public relations strategies of the local history collection working positively or negatively? Are the public relations activities reflecting the collection's objectives? Are the personnel responsible for the public relations activities doing an effective job?[7]

Public relations audits must be conducted with the assistance of top administrators of the local history collection and the parent library. Staff members should interview, in person, a sample of the local history collection's various publics: users, donors, administrators, staff members, and the news media—in-house and public.[8]

Questions regarding the local history collection focus on the interviewee's recognition of the collection and its programs. Can the interviewee give a correct description of the local history collection and its

LOUISIANA STATE UNIVERSITY

AND AGRICULTURAL AND MECHANICAL COLLEGE

T. Harry Williams Center for Oral History

INTERVIEWEE RELEASE FORM:

Tapes and Transcripts

I, _____, do hereby give to the T. Harry Williams
(name of interviewee)

Center all right, title or interest in the tape-recorded interviews conducted by

_____ on _____. I understand that
name of interviewer(s)   date(s)

these interviews will be protected by copyright and deposited in the LSU Libraries for

the use of future scholars. This gift does not preclude any use that I myself may want to

make of the information in these recordings.

CHECK ONE:

Tapes and transcripts may be used without restriction _____.

Tapes and transcripts are subject to the attached restrictions _____.

_____
Signature of Interviewee   Date

_____
Address

_____

_____
Telephone Number

_____
Director, T. Harry Williams Center

Hill Memorial Library • Baton Rouge • Louisiana • 70803-3300 • 504/388-6577 • FAX 504/388-6992

Fig. 7.5. Interviewee release form. Reprinted with permission of the T. Harry
Williams Center for Oral History, Louisiana State University.

activities? Has the interviewee read articles about the local history collection or seen advertisements for its programs? Have they attended an outreach program? If so, how would they rate the programs? Other questions should cite examples of some activities of the local history collection to determine if the interviewee had any awareness of the program.

Staff should review the answers to the interviewers' questions to find signs of strengths and weaknesses in the outreach and public relations activities of the local history collection. Evaluations can be used as guidelines to improving outreach programs and as an incentive to expand and refine these programs.

Many types of public relations and outreach programs are available to the local history collection. Excellent ideas appear in other collections' newsletters and journals of professional organizations like the American Association for State and Local History and the American Library Association. The key to success is planning. The staff should know what the resources of the local history collection are and seek a separate budget for public relations and outreach. If a separate budget is not available for these programs, public relations and outreach must be limited in size. The daily functions of the local history collection: acquiring, preserving, and making available local history materials are the most important activities. A public relations and outreach program that diminishes the quality of these programs will fail. Planners should keep proper records of all activities and evaluate each step of the way.

Whatever the shape or size of the local history collection's public relations and outreach program, they are an administrative responsibility based on staff resources; financial resources; support groups available; and the returned value to the collection, the parent library, and the community.

Notes

1. Lewis J. Bellardo and Lynn Lady Bellardo, comps., *A Glossary for Archivists, Manuscript Curators, and Records Managers* (Chicago: Society of American Archivists, 1992), 36.

2. Ann E. Pederson and Gail Farr Casterline, *Archives and Manuscripts: Public Programs* (Chicago: Society of American Archivists, 1982), 13.

3. Sylverna Ford, "The Library Newsletter, Is It for You?" *College and Research Libraries News* 49 (1988): 678-682.

4. Booklab, *BookNote 4: Safe Handling and Exhibition of Books* (Austin, TX: Booklab, not dated), 6.

5. See Sandy Dolnick, ed. *Friends of Libraries Source Book* (Chicago: American Library Association, 1990); Friends of Libraries, U.S.A., *The Best Ideas 1979-1989* (Bridgewater, NJ: Baker and Taylor, 1989).

6. Willa K. Baum, *Transcribing and Editing Oral History* (Nashville, TN: American Association for State and Local History, 1977); William W. Moss, *Oral History Program Manual* (New York: Praeger, 1974); Fredrick J. Stielow, *The Management of Oral History Sound Archives* (New York: Greenwood, 1986).

7. For example see Michael Haeuser and Evelyn Riche Olivier, "Effective Public Relations Programs Benefit Academic Libraries," *College and Research Libraries News* 50 (1989): 490-493.

8. Public Interest Public Relations, *Promoting Issues and Ideas: A Guide to Public Relations for Nonprofit Organizations* (New York: The Foundation Center, 1987), 13-16.

Administration of Local History Collections

Every local history collection, whether large or small, requires appropriate administration. Every organization, business, school, church, hospital, or library needs managers, and all managers need guidelines for managing. The local history collection manager requires policies and procedures, a staff, a budget, and a plan in order to properly administer the organization. This chapter seeks to outline in a simple way the basics needed for managing a local history collection. Management texts, manuals, and advice books are available for librarians, archivists, administrators, and volunteers. Readers should refer to appropriate texts for more in-depth discussion of management functions.[1] In spite of the endless amount of literature written about management, "the important principles of management are essentially simple and straightforward and their application is largely a matter of common sense."[2]

Policies and Procedures

Policies and procedures are essential for the local history collection to maintain consistency and provide the department with adequate administration. An up-to-date manual containing administrative policies and procedures for each function of the local history collection eliminates the need to make decisions on the same questions over and over. Once managers resolve a question, they write down the decision and make it a policy. The policy manual is a communication tool for all staff members. Procedures are necessary for each function, such as reference, processing manuscripts, cataloging, and acquisitions. Policy statements from the administrative parent of the local history collection, the library, are also maintained in the department. Policy is defined as "a verbal, written, or implied overall guide setting up boundaries that supply the general limits and direction in which managerial action will take place."[3]

Policies deal with each level of the organization. Personnel policies promulgated by the parent agency (the university, the city administration for public libraries, or the board of directors of a private organization) deal with employee hiring, firing, and evaluation. Personnel policies are part of the library administrative policy manual. Many policies of the parent institution are also affected by state and federal laws and are therefore inflexible until laws change. Policies come from outside and inside the organization and can be implied, imposed, or originated. Policies coming from outside the organization include state and federal laws that are essential to formulating in-house policy. Imposed policies are those created by state and federal laws such as copyright and minimum wage. For example, copyright in the United States is regulated by the Federal Copyright Act[4] (see chapter 6 for a full discussion of copyright).

Policies coming from inside the organization are those created by the organization itself. Implied policies are those that people assume are policies because of what goes on around them. For example, the administrator of an organization may receive first choice in the vacation schedule. While this is only tradition, not a policy, staff members may assume it is policy because it has always been done that way. Originated policies are those "developed to guide in the general operations of the library. These flow mainly from the objectives and are the main source of policy making within the organization."[5]

Policies for the local history collection, therefore, give the staff guidance in operating the collection. At what point should a staff member seek assistance from the department head for a difficult patron? What is the department policy on photocopying copyrighted materials? Under what circumstances may patrons view original items restricted because of physical condition? These are examples of policy questions. Procedures are "guides to action rather than guides to thinking, and they are subordinate to policies."[6] Policy sets how much time an employee receives for annual vacation, and procedures implement the policy. Procedures detail how vacation is applied for, how it is scheduled, and how records of leave are maintained.

A small local history collection may find that one procedures manual covers all functions. Larger collections need procedure manuals for each function of the department. Reference procedure manuals instruct staff how to "operate" the reference desk. For example, one set of procedures will explain exactly how patrons are allowed to request materials. Steps include: having the patron sign the daily register, fill out a registration form, read the user instructions, show a photo identification, and fill out a call slip for each item requested. The procedures manual is an excellent training tool for new staff members of the local history collection. New staff in cataloging should read the cataloging procedures manual, and new staff in reference should read the procedures manual for reference. Written procedures (no matter how simple) promote the consistency that dealing with the public and unique local history collection materials demands. When a procedure is changed, the procedures manual should be quickly updated and staff informed about the change. Changes occur when a better method for doing a specific task is developed, or when library policies dictate a change. Some managers are careful to change procedures only after consulting with and seeking the opinions of staff. Other managers make decisions to change procedures without staff consultation. However the decision is made, uninformed staff members cannot carry out changes in procedure. A written memo from the manager to the staff formally announcing procedure changes is a productive step.

Other functions of the local history collection also benefit from procedures manuals. Cataloging printed materials, processing archives and manuscripts and photographs, acquisitions and conservation require written procedures manuals to follow. Even small local history collections with only one or two staff members need written procedures manuals. Procedures are the methods whereby work is done most efficiently and productively for the local history collection.

Staffing

The local history collection staff may include several groups of workers, professionals, paraprofessionals, students, volunteers, and grant-funded employees. The local history collection within a library receives its staff allocations and money to pay for the staff from the library administration. The library administration can also determine what type of staff the collection receives. Some may be composed of one professional, one full-time or even part-time paraprofessional, and some volunteers. The Louisiana and Lower Mississippi Valley Collections of Louisiana State University is composed of five professional librarians/archivists, three and 3/4s paraprofessionals, one graduate assistant from the library school who works 20 hours per week, 160 hours per week of student assistant time, two grant-funded staff (one professional and one paraprofessional), and one volunteer. Staffing for the department changes with the number of grants funded, the number of qualified volunteers, and the amount of student assistant time allocated by the library administration. In most local history collections, professional staff supervise all other staff, and paraprofessionals supervise student and volunteer workers and other paraprofessionals.

What identifies professional and paraprofessional positions in the local history collection? Professional positions and the persons qualified to fill them are determined by library and parent organization policy. For most libraries in the United States, professional librarian positions require a master's degree in library and information science from a school accredited by the American Library Association. Professional archivist positions usually require a master's degree in an appropriate field (such as history) with archival administration training, or a master's degree in library science with archival courses or both. Some archival positions require a Ph.D. in an appropriate field, as do some librarian positions.

Whatever the level of the position—professional, paraprofessional, or clerical—each needs an accurate, up-to-date job description. If the parent organization of the library has a human resources department, that department will require job descriptions for all personnel. For small organizations that have no human resources or personnel departments, job descriptions for each position are still critical. During recruiting, prospective employees can better understand the requirements of the job by reviewing the position description, which should include the title of the position, the unit or department in which the position functions, the title of the person to whom the employee reports, the title of any people the position supervises, education and skills required for the position, and the tasks performed in the position.

Current personnel theory maintains that all tasks must be measurable in some manner. For example, a reference archivist might be required to answer 90 percent of all reference questions accurately. The manuscripts processing archivist might be required to produce finding aids to three collections each quarter. The objective, of course, is accountability. How well does the person perform the assigned tasks? The problem inherent in such a system is going so far to the extreme that professional responsibilities are demeaned to the quantifiable. When this happens, quality in performance suffers, sometimes even when quantity does not. Thus job descriptions must be written fairly, accurately, and comprehensively. A vague description of a task such as "works at the local history collection reference desk," is not acceptable. "To answer appropriate reference questions thoroughly and accurately in person, by telephone, or by letter" is an appropriate task description. Job descriptions also assist in yearly performance evaluations of staff. Personnel and human resources departments in large organizations require yearly performance evaluations for all personnel. Even small organizations benefit from implementing fair, careful, and thoughtful personnel evaluations, especially because many administrators use evaluations as a measure for merit salary raises. Most institutions develop or adapt performance evaluation measures and forms for their personnel.[7]

Performance Evaluations

Performance evaluations require candor on the part of the evaluator and the employee. Ignoring poor performance is unacceptable and counseling about poor performance is effective only when done frequently, not just once each year. Employees who perform poorly deserve an opportunity to improve performance through accurate evaluation at the earliest time after a problem is observed. It is the supervisor's responsibility to ensure that employees are aware of their performance ratings at all times. Each employee should be given monthly, or even weekly, opportunities to discuss job performance with the supervisor. If an employee performs poorly, and timely evaluations do not improve performance, the employee probably will need to be terminated.

If supervisors and employees discuss performance on a regular basis, then annual, formal performance evaluations become painless. While supervisors are required to follow the personnel procedures of their organization, management consultant Peter Drucker's comments about performance evaluations prove useful to quality evaluations. Drucker, in discussing performance "appraisals" in 1966, emphasized that they tended to focus on the negatives—what is wrong with the employee. Drucker suggests that performance appraisals look at the "major contributions expected . . . in . . . past

and present positions and a record . . . performance against these goals."
Further, he suggests four questions to be considered:

(a) "What has he [or she] done well?"
(b) "What, therefore, is he [or she] likely to be able to do well?"
(c) "What does he [or she] have to learn or to acquire to be able to get the full benefit from his [or her] strength?"
(d) "If I had a son or daughter, would I be willing to have him or her work under this person?"
    (i) "If yes, why?"
    (ii) "If no, why?"

This appraisal actually takes a much more critical look at a [person] than the usual procedure does. But it focuses on strengths. It begins with what a [person] can do. Weaknesses are seen as limitations to the full use of his [or her] strengths and to his [or her] own achievement, effectiveness, and accomplishment."[8]

Performance evaluations are also critical to the effectiveness of students, volunteers, and grant-funded employees. (For a discussion of volunteer workers in the local history collection see chapter 6.) While the evaluations for students and volunteers are not as extensive as those for full-time employees, the grant-funded worker receives the same evaluation as a regular worker.

Student employee performance evaluations assist in the learning process for students by helping them to develop the skills and knowledge needed for their first job beyond school. Working in the local history collection is a part of the learning experience for students. Fortunate university and college libraries have a budget for student workers, including some paid from special funds such as work-study programs. Most students have little work experience, few skills, and limited hours to work. However, they are a great asset if managed properly. One person should supervise the student workers in each unit. That staff member should handle time cards, complaints, training, scheduling, and evaluations. Student supervisors should maintain policy and procedures manuals for students. Each new student worker benefits from reading and becoming familiar with the policies and procedures of the local history collection and the parent institution.

Work assigned to students is mostly clerical and involves assisting full-time staff. Tasks often assigned to students include being pages for the reference desk, rehousing manuscripts and archives, staffing an information desk, reshelving, filing, preparing reading room statistical reports, making book jackets, cutting mats for exhibits, answering the phone, and clerical work. Student workers who gain such experience may become the next generation of local history collection professionals.

As with students and volunteers, grant-funded employees are probably short term workers. Depending on the type of grant and amount received, the local history collection may hire specialized workers for a limited period of time to complete the grant project. Such workers may be professional, paraprofessional, or clerical. Their compensation is based on the amount received and specified in the grant. Although grant funds are probably administered through the business office of the parent organization, the local history collection is usually permitted to hire the employee for the grant-funded position. For grants lasting two to three years, the local history collection will have time to advertise in national professional publications. For shorter term grants, qualified personnel can sometimes be recruited at the local level. Tasks assigned to the grant-funded employee must be clearly defined. A job description for a grant-funded position is often required by the granting agency and is used for recruiting employees. Grant-funded employees need to be evaluated on the specific tasks of the grant. Also, because grant-funded employees tend to be short-term, they may feel isolated from other staff and the workings of the local history collection as a whole. These employees benefit from being included in all departmental meetings and given opportunities to review policy and procedures manuals.

Permanent staff also perform better if encouraged to be part of a professionally active team. Staff receive continuing education and bring increased knowledge to the job from active professional involvement. Organizations such as the Society of American Archivists, the American Library Association, and the American Association for State and Local History provide staff with professional literature, workshops, yearly conferences, and a network of colleagues. These organizations have publishing departments that provide extensive professional literature to local history collections staff. Some staff members will also belong to scholarly organizations representing their individual interests such as preservation organizations, folklore societies, anthropological associations, historical societies, and oral history associations. Finally, the local history collection employee may find it useful to belong to local and state professional associations. The benefits to the local history collection are broadened education for staff, contact with potential researchers, and a wider network of colleagues.

Planning

Managing an effective and efficient local history collection takes planning. All staff, including professional, paraprofessional, managers, and administrators, must be involved in the planning process in order for it to succeed. Planning for the next year begins when the current annual report is written. Goals and the strategies to meet those goals are a part of every yearly plan. Like a collection development policy, a set of goals and objectives serves as a road map for the local history collection. Each annual report should study which goals were met during the previous year and why or why not. Then new goals should be identified based on what has already been accomplished and what still needs to be done.

The two greatest mistakes made in planning are refusing to plan and setting goals that are unrealistic. Planning is one of the least frequently performed of all management activities, and the reasons are varied. Most often, staff members claim they have no time to plan. But this is a plan in itself.

Taking no action is a choice and usually the wrong one. Haphazard management and crisis management fill the void created by a lack of planning. The second basic problem with planning is setting goals that cannot be achieved. Local history collection development policies and documentation standards assist staff in yearly planning. Goals can be reached by using short-term strategies according to a plan. If the long-range goal is to improve the quality and quantity of research materials in the local history collection, then a short-term strategy for reaching that goal may be to increase gift book acquisitions by ten percent. To achieve this goal, individual staff members are assigned tasks related to acquiring more gift books for the collection. Such tasks may include soliciting gifts from donors or establishing a program to swap duplicate gift books with another local history collection or library. The larger goal of improving the research materials is feasible when a plan that outlines various steps to achieving that goal is adopted.

To combat the mistakes of failing to plan and adopting unachievable goals, set aside time to plan and develop realistic goals. While finding the time may seem impossible at first, after making planning a habit, it becomes easier and easier. This is, of course, incumbent on finding a location to work in which outside disturbances are minimized. Monthly reports should include planning for the next month. Realistic goals can be established by reviewing the work of the local history collection. What does the staff do? How do they do it? Can the work of the staff be improved? How and why? Staff and administration need to find time for successful and positive planning.

Successful, positive planning consists of short range and long range goals. Long range plans (strategic plans) are those that reflect the status of programs five or ten years ahead. For example, the Society of American Archivists published *Planning for the Archival Profession: A Report of the SAA Task Force on Goals and Priorities* in 1986. This report is an excellent model for long-range planning. All of the elements of running the organization must be taken into account when doing long-range planning. The mission of the organization, the collection development policies, budget, staffing, and short-range (or yearly) plans. In the long-range plan of the library, a goal may be to increase grant funding by 50 percent over a five-year period. In turn, the local history collection will be expected to be part of increasing the total dollar amount of grant funding received by the library over a five year period. Long-range planning attempts to develop a realistic plans for the future of the organization.

Most long-range or strategic planning is defined by Drucker as "the continuous process of making present entrepreneurial (risk-taking) decisions systematically and with the greatest knowledge of their futurity; organizing systematically the efforts needed to carry out these decisions; and measuring the results of these decisions against the expectations through organized, systematic feedback."[9]

Long-range planning is not an exercise in prognostication, but a plan of action based on known trends and economics. Public librarians are currently facing a trend of decreasing financial support from the federal sector. In turn, less money is available from state and local sectors because more tax money must go to cover other federal cutbacks. Inner city libraries are faced with budget cuts caused by eroding tax bases. University libraries are unable to purchase large amounts of foreign materials because the dollar buys less. While local history collection managers may not be able to devise a long-range plan outside the goals of the parent library, they must be prepared to develop a plan for the local history collection that will become part of the library's long-range plan.[10]

A short-range plan is usually a yearly plan and may coincide with the yearly budget plan. Long-range plans tend to be very broad and general, while short-range plans need to be specific. These plans reflect specifically what is to be accomplished during the year ahead based on the funds allocated to the local history collection. The short-range plan within a given year may be to improve the quality of research collections by preserving and cataloging a noted photography collection. To achieve this goal, the local history collection administrator and photograph archivist write a grant proposal to the National Endowment for the Humanities' Division of Preservation and Access. The local history collection staff work with library administrators, the conservation department of the library, and other appropriate departments in planning the grant proposal. If the grant is received, an objective for the following year will be to carry out the grant project in the local history collection.

Long-range and short-range planning benefits everyone in the library and the community. This is hard to see when staff are overworked, underpaid, and the backlog of uncataloged materials and uncollected acquisitions grows each day. How does planning help? Planning creates an opportunity to review the daily activities of the local history collection and consider why they exist and why they do or do not work. Planning for the upcoming year and reviewing the activities of the past year assist the local history collection staff in determining why some projects are not being completed and other activities are very successful. Planning that involves all local history collection staff gives the department, as a whole, an investment in the success of the activities planned. Planning is a road map to follow. Careful, well produced plans can create a local history collection that defies cutting or dismantling in times of financial duress. We must all plan to plan.

Budgeting

A large segment of planning is budgeting. Each local history collection requires money to operate, and most monies come from the budget allocated each year from the parent organization. The local history collection within the library may or may not receive a distinct, separate budget. In many libraries, for example, the local history collection is part of the special collections division, which receives a budget allocation for each year. The local history collection then receives its allocation from the special collections division. In this organizational arrangement, the local history collection staff is asked to prepare a complete budget each year, including costs for staff, costs for special supplies, costs for office supplies, and costs for acquisitions. However, some local history collections simply function as a separate unit, budget-wise, from the other special collections. In such cases, all units of special collections have the same supply budget, under which all special archival and preservation supplies are purchased. Each unit uses supplies from the central supply area as needed. Each unit is asked each year to develop a supply request list, but does not have a separate budget allocation. Allocation for staff is from the parent organization to the library, and all staff positions are allocated through the library administration. This creates a more flexible staffing pattern wherein the library assigns staff to the various departments as needed.

The other extreme of the budgeting spectrum is when the local history collection is required to prepare a yearly budget for each function: staffing, supplies, office equipment, travel, telephone, photocopying services, and outreach. Budgeting is considered a control and planning device by administrators in profit and nonprofit agencies. Budgeting for the profit corporation is affected by the so-called "bottom-line," that is, whether the budget creates a situation whereby the company makes a profit or not. If the company does not make a profit, managers assume budget adjustments are needed. For example, when profits are high, more money goes to research and development, but when profits are down, staff are eliminated temporarily or permanently. Profit margins do not affect nonprofit organizations, but budgets are still used as planning and controlling devices. When patron use of the local history collection increases, the administrator may request more money for public service staff. The increase in use may have grown out of a planned increase in public relations and outreach services just the year before. So, if the local history collection administrator plans properly, money allocated to increased activities in one are may lead to a planned increase in staff for another area. A budget defines the manager's authority to act within stated goals and objectives.[11] Authority to act, to carry out planned programs and activities, is critically important to the manager. Otherwise, the local history collection could become a castoff in times of budget constraints and cutbacks.

Young local history collections established in flush economic times were probably seen as positive new programs. Or the local history collection may be older than the parent library, having been started by the local historical society before a public library existed in the town. Whatever the case, deeds of gifts and deposit are part of the administrative responsibilities of the local history collection staff (see chapter 2 for a discussion of deeds of gift). These deeds insure the donor of materials to the local history collection that the items will be cared for and made available for research use. Strong public relations with the community assure that dismantling the local history collection would be a difficult choice in severe financial times. Also, a substantial number of users in relationship to the size of the collection is critical to maintaining the local history collection during a recession. Like the product that does not make a profit for the corporation, a program that does not meet its planned goals is easier for the parent organization to cut.

Even though the local history collection administrator may not be required to complete elaborate budget requests each year, every local history collection librarian and archivist needs to know the basics of accurate budgeting. The first rule is to understand where the money comes from and how it is allocated. The parent library may use one type of budget or a combination of several types. The most common types of budgets for libraries and local history collections are line item, lump sum, formula, program, performance, Planning Programming budgeting system (PPBS), and Zero Based Budgeting (ZBB) (see fig. 8.1). Whatever the type of budget used, the local history collection manager must understand it and the ramifications of its use in order to be as effective as possible. Many librarians and archivists receive a brief introduction to budgeting in management courses they take in graduate school. Their personal libraries probably contain a basic guide to management and budgeting. Continuing education courses in management, budgeting, and planning with assist the librarian or archivist who aspires to be a manager.

BUDGET DEFINITIONS

Line item   divides expenditures into broad categories, such as salaries and wages, materials and supplies, equipment, capital expenditures, and miscellaneous.

Lump sum   a certain dollar amount allocation, which the receiving agency must break into categories.

Formula budgets   use predetermined standards for allocation of monetary resources. These formulae are usually expressed in terms of a percentage of the total institutional cost.

Program budget   dollars are assigned to programs and/or services provided. This budget is concerned with the organization's activities, not with individual items or expenditures.

Performance budgeting   bases expenditures on the performance of activities and emphasizes efficiency of operations.

Planning Programming Budgeting System (PPBS)   begins with the establishment of goals and objectives, emphasizing the cost of accomplishing goals set by the library instead of stressing objects.

Zero Based Budgeting (ZBB)   requires that justification for each program start from point "zero" in the discussions each year and is not concerned with what happened previously, but rather with what is required in the future.

Fig. 8.1. Budget definitions. From Robert D. Stueart and Barbara B. Moran, *Library Management*, 3d ed. (Englewood, CO: Libraries Unlimited, 1987), 206-218.

As the library budget pie grows smaller and smaller, local history collections need to look for innovative ways to raise extra funds for their programs and activities. One of the best is to apply for a grant. Federal grants come from the National Endowment for the Humanities (NEH), the

National Endowment for the Arts (NEA), the National Historical Publications and Records Commission (NHPRC), the National Science Foundation (NSF), the Higher Education Act, and others (see fig. 8.2). The key to securing a grant from these agencies is to follow their procedures and guidelines to the letter. Many times, grants are not funded because the applicant forgot to include something as simple as a work plan for the project for which they were applying. Staff should seek the assistance of a colleague who has been successful in receiving grants. Also, the staffs of NEH and NHPRC encourage telephone calls to discuss prospective grants before the applicant sends in the final proposal. Communication with the granting agency eliminates many mistakes and makes sure the applicant is on target.

FEDERAL GRANT AGENCIES

National Endowment for the Humanities (NEH)
1100 Pennsylvania Avenue, N.W.
Washington, DC 20506
(202) 786-0570

National Historical Publications and Records Commission (NHPRC)
National Archives and Records Administration
Washington, DC 20408
(202) 501-5610

Department of Education
555 New Jersey Avenue, N.W., Room 404
Washington, DC 20208
(202) 219-1315

Institute of Museum Services
1100 Pennsylvania Avenue, N.W., Room 609
Washington, DC 20506
(202) 786-0539

National Endowment for the Arts (NEA)
1100 Pennsylvania Avenue, N.W., Room 624
Washington, DC 20506
(202) 682-5442

National Science Foundation (NSF)
1800 G Street, N.W.
Washington, DC 20550
(202) 357-7075

Fig. 8.2. Federal grant agencies.

Local grant agencies may also donate money to local history collections. Each state has a component of the NEA and the NEH. These are usually titled with the state name, such as the Louisiana Endowment for the Humanities and the Louisiana Endowment for the Arts. These agencies provide grants, but on a much smaller scale than the national agencies. The Louisiana Endowment for the Humanities, for example, is concerned with broadening adult knowledge of the humanities. Therefore, it only funds projects that include public programs on humanities topics for the out-of-school adult community. The state endowment will pay for exhibitions that also have a public program that includes a humanities scholar speaking on the subjects the exhibition covers. The Louisiana Endowment for the Humanities will not pay for purely in-house projects, such as cataloging a pamphlet or map collection. Other local and state grant agencies may be connected to local businesses or state charitable trusts. The Pew Charitable Trust is well-known in Pennsylvania, and the bulk of their grant money goes to projects in Pennsylvania. Other foundations are local and give money on a very limited basis. The administrator should check reference books that give information on private foundations and granting agencies to determine which organizations are appropriate for the local history collection to apply to. Further information on granting agencies can be found in the Foundation Center's *Foundation Directory* and database available at library reference departments.

The first question the local history collection staff should ask before writing a grant application is, can we really afford this grant? Grants are never free. To obtain a grant, the local history collection is required to provide cost sharing. Cost sharing items allowed by federal agencies vary, but most will allow for the percentage of time that staff of the collection will allocate to the grant and the fringe benefits that staff receives, equipment and supplies, and some other types of items. Some agencies will even allow for indirect costs, that is, the cost of electricity and office space within the institution. Some agencies require cost sharing of 50 percent of the total of the grant application; some require no cost sharing. Staff must consult the guidelines of the granting agency for cost sharing rules. Indirect cost rates negotiated by nonprofit organizations require elaborate financial reporting. Most colleges, universities, and public libraries negotiate these amounts once every several years with the proper federal agency. The grants and contracts office of the parent agency should inform departments of the indirect cost rate. For those local history collections whose parent institutions have a grants and contract office, the application process as well as the grant are monitored by that office. Such grants and contracts offices are very useful in preventing budgeting mistakes and should be used by the local history collection staff.

As part of the cost sharing for a grant, local history collection staff time can be included. Can the local history collection allocate ten or 20 percent of a staff member's time to grant activities? If the grant will allow the collection to hire special grant-funded staff, is there a proper place for the extra person to work? Are supplies adequate to meet the needs of the grant-funded staff or will the cost of supplies be included in the grant? Who on the local history collection staff has the necessary time to devote to writing a grant proposal? These are a few of the necessary questions to ask before applying for a grant. Grant funds are excellent ways for local history collections to implement new projects and to help broaden and finish ongoing projects if they can afford the grant.

How do local history collections determine when to apply for grants and to whom? Grants are usually seen as a way to pay for a project that otherwise would not be done. The NEH's United States Newspaper Project has funded millions of dollars in grant projects pertaining to the preservation of newspapers in the 50 states. The projects require that a state agency, such as a state historical society, locate and microfilm all existing newspapers printed in the state. Other grants pay for cataloging the newspaper microfilm and for creating a guide to all the newspapers. Because of the United States Newspaper Project, most of the states now have a listing on OCLC for microfilm of newspapers in each state. This is, of course, of great service to all researchers and to each state. Smaller grants for the local history collection also serve a vast number of researchers.

The NEH has recently funded the arrangement and description of regionally or nationally significant manuscript collections and guides to them. The NEH sometimes pays for microfilming the papers, as well. The microfilm can be sold to other libraries and to researchers, thus extending the use of the manuscripts. NHPRC has funded grants to universities to establish university archives. The U.S. Office of Education, which funds Title IIC grants, has supported projects to catalog materials printed in the Confederacy during the Civil War. The staff member planning grant projects should contact all agencies that might be applied to for a grant and compile a file of their guidelines and application procedures. This file should be updated periodically, or whenever the agency announces program changes. A file on ideas for projects that might be appropriate for grant funding is also a helpful planning tool. All staff must be aware that some grant agencies take as much as a year to review applications and to allocate funds, realize that the competition for grants is very strong, and that only clearly written grant proposals receive funding. If the grant application is poorly written and unclear, no number of distinguished letters of support will cause the grant to be funded. Local history collections managers should practice writing grant proposals and devising grant budgets; attend a grant writing workshop locally or at a professional meeting; and read professional newsletters to learn who is funding what type of grants. While acquiring grant funds is difficult, it is not impossible.

Building an endowment is another way to establish extra funding for the local history collection. Within the framework of the parent institution, some staff member is responsible for working with donors who wish to contribute money to the institution. Such funds are usually allocated to an endowment fund. The funds are deposited, and the interest earned from the funds is spent by the institution to fund special projects or defray operating expenses. Endowments may bear the name of the donor or the name of the local history collection. Local history collection staff and administrators work to interest donors in adding to the endowment fund. In some years, it may be best to reinvest the interest earned by the account into the principal in order to build up the interest earning amount. If the parent institution has no financial planning office, propose a program whereby an endowment can be established for the local history collection. The friends of the local history collection or the friends of the library are excellent organizations to develop special funding programs.

Local history collections are vital parts of many research, education, historical society, museum, and corporation libraries. They perform a service for citizens of all ages and with varied research interests. Their proper development, operation, preservation, and management is an important responsibility. Giving guidance in performing these functions well is the hope of those involved in presenting this manual.

Notes

1. See Robert D. Stueart and Barbara B. Moran, *Library Management*, 3d ed. (Englewood, CO: Libraries Unlimited, 1987); and Thomas Wilsted and William Nolte, *Managing Archival and Manuscript Repositories* (Chicago: Society of American Archivists, 1991).

2. James C. Worthy, "Management Concepts and Archival Administration," in *A Modern Archives Reader: Basic Readings on Archival Theory and Practice*, Maygene Daniels and Timothy Walch, eds. (Washington, DC: National Archives and Records Service, 1984), 308.

3. M. Valliant Higginson, "Putting Policies in Context," in *Business Policy*, Alfred Gross and Walter Gross, eds. (New York: Ronald Press, 1967), 230.

4. U.S. Code Title 17, write to the Register of Copyrights, Library of Congress, Washington, DC 21059.

5. Stueart and Moran, *Library Management,* 43.

6. Ibid., 45.

7. Ibid., 100-105, for a discussion of job descriptions and performance evaluations in libraries.

8. Peter F. Drucker, *The Effective Executive* (New York: Harper & Row, 1967), 86; see also Barbara Williams Jenkins and Mary L. Smalls, *Performance Appraisal in Academic Libraries* CLIP Note #12 (Chicago: Association of College and Research Libraries, 1990).

9. Peter F. Drucker, *Management* (New York: Harper & Row, 1974), 25.

10. For an excellent discussion of long-range, strategic planning see Siri N. Espy, *Handbook of Strategic Planning for Nonprofit Organizations* (New York: Praeger Publishers, 1986).

11. Stueart and Moran, *Library Management,* 204.

Appendix A
Louisiana and Lower Mississippi Valley Collections
Collection Development Policy Statement

Reprinted with permission of the Louisiana and Lower Mississippi Valley Collections, LSU Libraries, Louisiana State University.

I. <u>Statement of Purpose</u>:
The Louisiana and Lower Mississippi Valley Collection (LLMVC) is a department within the Special Collections division of the LSU Libraries. The primary mission of the LSU Libraries is to serve the teaching, research, and public service needs of the University and the scholarly community. The role of the LLMVC in accomplishing this mission is to collect, preserve, and make available for research materials relating primarily to the history and culture of Louisiana and the lower Mississippi Valley region.

II. <u>Types of Programs Supported by the Collection</u>:
    A. **Research** Materials collected and made available shall further the research of LSU faculty, staff, and students, Louisianians, and visiting scholars in the history and culture of Louisiana and the lower Mississippi Valley region. In order to support all levels of research, the LLMVC shall seek to provide exhaustive resources on the history and culture of Louisiana and lower Mississippi Valley region, achievements of Louisianians, as well as materials that build on current strengths.
    B. **Preservation and Security** Crucial to the ongoing operation of the Special Collections program is the preservation of research materials. Collections are stored in acid-free containers in Hill Memorial Library, which features a temperature and humidity controlled environment and fire detection and suppression systems. The LLMVC is a non-circulating collection that is maintained in closed stacks. Security measures include security personnel, and an alarm system that is monitored by the LSU Police Department.
    C. **Exhibitions** As part of the overall Special Collections program, the LLMVC mounts on a rotating basis, exhibitions featuring and interpreting materials from the collections. The exhibition areas consist of free standing and wall-mounted exhibit cases. Exhibitions are prepared by Special Collections staff, under the coordination of the head of the Rare Book Collections. Special Collections will consider requests to loan unrestricted materials and facsimiles for exhibition to other research institutions when the policies and facilities of those institutions meet acceptable standards and proper credit is given to the LSU Libraries.

133

D. **Outreach and Publications** The LLMVC seeks to further the use and development of the collections through an outreach program that increases public awareness of the nature and relevance of the collections. This program includes exhibitions (see II.C.), tours of the LLMVC facilities and presentations by the head and staff of LLMVC; and publications such as brochures, catalogs, and a newsletter. Awareness of the collections among the scholarly community will be fostered by entering information about the collections in national databases, such as RLIN; reporting them to national lists, such as the National Union Catalog of Manuscript Collections; and publicizing acquisitions in the news media and professional, scholarly, and popular publications.

E. **Acquisitions** The LLMVC acquires materials through donation, loan and deposit, and purchase. Purchases are financed by legislatively appropriated funds in the LSU Libraries acquisitions budget; by income from endowment funds; and by cash donations. Donations of materials and funds are essential to maintaining and developing the collections, and the support of donors is consistently sought. Grant funding for special projects will be sought when such projects do not diminish the level of routine care and service of the collections, and when they can contribute substantially to the acquisition, arrangement and description, or servicing of the collections.

III. Clientele Served by the Collections:
The policy of the LLMVC is to make materials available to researchers on equal terms, subject to the appropriate care and handling of the materials by the researcher.

A. **Scholars** University faculty and staff and non-LSU faculty are permitted to use the LLMVC with proper identification and registration.

B. **Graduate and Undergraduate Students** III.A. also applies to University and non-LSU graduate and undergraduate students.

C. **General Public** Members of the general public are welcome to use the LLMVC with proper identification and registration.

D. **High School Students** High school students are granted use of the LLMVC with proper identification and registration if accompanied by a guardian.

IV. Priorities and Limitations of the Collection:
A. **Present Collections Strength** The LLMVC is strongest in the areas of Southern political economy (1800-present), antebellum life and culture, plantation life and culture, Southern agriculture, slavery, the Civil War, 19th century Southern business history, twentieth century Louisiana politics, and history of the University.

B. **Present Collecting Level** The LLMVC covers the history, literature, economy, politics, and culture of Louisiana, the lower Mississippi Valley region, and the South, with emphasis on: French and Spanish colonial periods; early English and ethnic settlements; war, particularly the Civil War; antebellum and postbellum life and culture; transportation; agriculture; writers; families; pre-20th century women; 20th century regional political leaders and organizations; slavery; black life and culture;

banking; lumber, sugar, cotton, moss, seafood, oil, fur, and other indigenous industries; and social, cultural, and educational organizations. The LLMVC also preserves official records of the University and the papers of LSU faculty, staff, students, alumni, and organizations.

    C. **Present Identified Weaknesses** The LLMVC is weak in certain areas of the 20th century history, particularly as relates to women, minorities, and ethnic groups, which the LLMVC will aggressively collect.

    D. **Desired Level of Collecting** As a major research center on Louisiana, the LLMVC will exhaustively and aggressively collect all materials that pertain to the history and culture of Louisiana and the lower Mississippi Valley region, as specified in IV.B and IV.C., including materials written by and about Louisianians and published in Louisiana.

    E. **Geographic Areas Collected** Louisiana, colonial French and Spanish Louisiana territories, Mississippi, lower Mississippi Valley region below Memphis, and the border areas of Arkansas and Texas.

    F. **Chronological Periods Collected** No limitations; primarily 19th and 20th centuries.

    G. **Subject Areas Collected** The LLMVC collects materials in all subject areas, as specified in IV.B. and IV.C., with particular emphasis given to economic, social, cultural, political, literary, and military history.

    H. **Languages Collected** The LLMVC collects materials primarily in the English language, but also accepts those languages indigenous to Louisiana, particularly French, and including Spanish, German, Italian, and their respective dialects.

    I. **Forms of Material Collected** The LLMVC is an integrated collection that acquires material in all formats, including monographs, manuscripts, archives, maps, photographs, pamphlets, state government documents, audio-visual materials, microforms, prints, machine readable records, newspapers, sheet music, oral history, and selected memorabilia.

    J. **Exclusions** - The LLMVC will not generally accept the following: Materials that reflect the history of a geographical area other than that listed in IV.E.; partial manuscript and archival collections when major portions of the collection have already been deposited in another repository; and collections of purely genealogical material, with the exception of Louisiana publications.

V.   <u>Cooperative Agreements Affecting the Collecting Policy</u>:
The LLMVC recognizes that other institutions collect in the same or overlapping areas, and will seek to acquire similar unique resources for their own collections. The LLMVC also recognizes that other institutions may have prior claim on such materials or be a more appropriate repository to house them. Opportunities to acquire such materials, as well as those not covered by the LLMVC collecting policy, will be referred to an appropriate repository. In cases where the legitimate collecting interests of the LLMVC and another repository directly conflict, the LLMVC will use the best interest of the scholarly community as a criterion in pursuing a resolution.

VI.   Statements of Resource Sharing Policy:
The LLMVC will consider requests to microfilm materials for inclusion in another repository, subject to specific limitations imposed by the terms of acquisition, and subject to the routine photoduplication policy of the LLMVC.

VII.   Statement of Deaccessioning Policy:
Duplicates and materials that do not reflect the collecting areas of the LLMVC may be deaccessioned, subject to the terms of acquisition, University regulations, and state and federal laws, and offered to other more appropriate institutions or the donor or donor's family.

VIII.   Procedures Affecting Collecting Policy and Its Expedition:
   A. **Deed of Gift** The LLMVC will not accept materials without a legal transfer of title, deed of gift or deposit, or other official acknowledgment.
   B. **Loans and Deposits** Materials loaned to or deposited with the LLMVC will be accepted when the conditions for acceptance are favorable to the LSU Libraries.
   C. **Closed Collections** The LLMVC will not ordinarily accept collections of materials that are closed to public access in perpetuity.
   D. **Deaccessioning** The LLMVC reserves the right to deaccession any materials within its collections, subject to the terms of acquisition and the notification of the donor or his/her heirs.
   E. **Exhibitions** The LLMVC reserves the right to include unrestricted materials in exhibitions, in accordance with normally accepted archival principles and practices.
   F. **Revision of Policies** The LLMVC reserves the right to change the preceding policies without notification to heirs.

IX.   Procedures for Monitoring Development and Reviewing Collection Development Guidelines:
This collecting policy is designed to meet the goals of the LSU Libraries, the Special Collections Division, and the Louisiana and Lower Mississippi Valley Collections. In order to determine the effectiveness of the collecting policy, at the end of every academic year, the staff will review the acquisitions, user records, and deaccessions of the preceding fiscal year. The policy will be re-evaluated and changed as needed to meet the goals of the LSU Libraries and Louisiana State University and Agricultural and Mechanical College.

Appendix B
Sample Documentation Strategy

Documenting the Nineteenth Century
History of Somewhere, USA

Somewhere, USA, is a small suburban town of 25,000 residents that was founded in 1803 by a now-defunct religious sect. The first industry in the town was a lumber mill and yard, which still operates. Other 19th century industries were a cotton mill, a furniture manufacturing plant, and a machine shop. Current industries are an automobile parts manufacturing plant, a clothing manufacturer, and a computer chip assembly plant. Five families of English descent first settled in the area, and descendants of those families still live in Somewhere. A Native American tribe has resided in the area since prehistory and is a viable force in the town today. Of the five churches formed in the 19th century, four are currently active; and one new church has been formed in the 20th century. In the 19th century, small groups of Italian, Greek, and African immigrants settled in Somewhere. Because of its location, the town was minimally affected by the American Civil War, but has numerous veterans of 20th century wars. Public education began in the town in 1845; prior to that time, education was the responsibility of church schools. In 1863 a private, nonchurch affiliated girls' school was established in the town and existed until 1955. Several famous Americans were graduates of the girls' school. In 1960 a community college was established, which is part of the state university system. The first public library was established in 1850, and the local history collection began in 1902. Over the years the town has had the usual small businesses and organizations common to American towns.

Steps to be taken in the documentation strategy:
1. Review of current collection development policies.
2. Questions included as part of the strategy:

   a. **What materials exist that document the history of Somewhere, USA, from its founding in 1803 to 1900?** Examples: records of the religious sect that founded the town; papers of the first families of the town; records of the private girls' school existing in the town from 1863 to 1955; papers of the 19th century town historian; records of the local tribal council in the 19th century; oral traditions of the local Native American tribe; oral traditions of other ethnic groups in the community; church records; other (the local history collection staff has decided to prepare a separate documentation strategy for local government records).

   b. **Which materials are not available and why?** Perform a records survey to determine if the papers and records of the individuals and groups in the above list exist. Compile a list of those that warrant further investigation and those which do not. Example 1: The local history collection wishes to acquire the papers of the Reverend Smith Jones's family. Rev. Smith Jones was the first Baptist minister to settle in Somewhere, arriving in 1842 and overseeing the building of the First Baptist Church in 1845. Rev. Jones's family was very close-knit, and children, grandchildren, and cousins lived within 100 miles of each other. In 1952, a great-grandson of Rev. Jones began to compile a genealogy of the family. He gathered papers, photographs, scrapbooks, and other materials from all family members. Upon completing his history in 1960, he stored all the family papers in his barn. After years of negotiation, the local history collection staff received permission to retrieve the materials from the barn. Water, mildew, mold, rats, bugs, dogs, and cats had completely destroyed all but one cubic foot box of the 100 boxes of materials. On the local history collection family papers survey, the Rev. Smith Jones's family papers are listed as destroyed. No further searching for papers from the family will be done.

Example 2: A portion of the records of the local girls' school were found by historic building preservationists in the building in which the school resided. The records found cover from 1863, the year of the school's founding, to 1880. Other records are missing, but information in the records indicates that traditionally the principal's secretary was responsible for the records. The last secretary, who was also the principal's wife, may have taken the records from 1880 to 1955. Therefore, it is noted on the records survey that staff should continue to search for the records of the school.

c. **How can materials be made available?** List people who own the materials, assign a staff member or advisory committee member to visit them, discuss the materials and the work of the local history collection, and begin negotiations for the transfer of materials to the local history collection. [If the strategy were for 20th century records of functioning organizations, this step would include providing a records management plan for the organization.]

d. **What are the uses and benefits of materials for the local area?** Possible ways the papers might be used include local histories, student papers, documentary films, radio programs, research for the living history museum, genealogies, and novels. Benefits to the community include collecting information useful in legal research, promoting pride in the community, and preserving community histories. The local history collection should develop public relations brochures, flyers, and other items that show the value of preserving materials in the collection.

e. **Who is interested in the documentation of the area?** Those interested will eventually include most citizens, once the project is publicized. Those interested in beginning the project might include teachers, school board members, town council members, local historians, genealogical society members, and leading business people. Some of these individuals should form the documentation strategy advisory committee.

f. **What current activities and actions are detrimental to full documentation?** Examples are improper storage of materials; misuse of materials, such as nonarchival displays; owners who refuse access to the materials; owners asking exorbitant prices for purchase of materials; materials being sold to nonlocal research collections; and noncooperation of citizens with the local history collection. [If the strategy were for 20th century material, this might include the lack of a records management program for the organization, the destruction of family papers by their descendants, or the lack of correspondence written by 20th century families.]

g. **What can be done to improve documentation?** The local history collection can improve publicity, have continued re-evaluation of the documentation strategy, develop guidelines for citizens to use in caring for family papers, meet regularly with town government officials, and develop other outreach activities.

3. Establish a documentation strategy implementation group. Consider including those who have expressed interest in the project, and seek out others vital to the success of the project. These may include local business people, officers of local organizations, teachers, college faculty members, members of local ethnic groups, local government officials, and students. A good cross section of the community would be most valuable. The committee should be of a workable size (10-15 members) and must be an active working group, not an honorary group.

4. Write the documentation strategy for dissemination to local citizens. A small flyer is an excellent way to do this. The above questions should be included on the flyer, with the local history collections telephone number and address, and the names of contact people.

5. Once the strategy and the committee are in place, updates on progress of the strategy should be given to the committee for their review. The committee's purpose is to assist in complete documentation of the town, not to revise policies and procedures of the local history collection. Committee members may be asked to assist in records surveys and family papers surveys.

6. Keep complete records of the activities of the committee and the progress of the project. All files on the project become part of the library's archives.

7. The strategy to document the 19th century history of Somewhere, USA, will be an ongoing process that may be continued by the staff of the local history collection for many years. However, the work of the committee should be limited to a certain time period. One to two years may be adequate for their work. At the completion of the work of the committee, the local history collection staff will begin another documentation strategy project. Other areas for documentation may include: local government, local Native American tribal council, religious organizations, businesses, civic groups, education, ethnic groups, industrial development, and many others.

NOTE: In addition to the articles by Samuels and Hackman and Warnow-Blewett, the Society of American Archivists has published other case studies of documentation strategies. Included are: the articles in the *American Archivist* 50 (Fall 1987); and Richard J. Cox, "A Documentation Strategy Case Study: Western New York," *American Archivist* 52 (Spring 1989): 192-201.

Appendix C

MARSHALL-FURMAN FAMILY PAPERS

(Mss 4042, 2740)

Inventory

Compiled by

Sally C. Proshek

Louisiana and Lower Mississippi Valley Collections
Special Collections, Hill Memorial Library
Louisiana State University Libraries
Baton Rouge, Louisiana

April 1991

MARSHALL-FURMAN FAMILY PAPERS
1794-1975

Contents of Inventory

Summary	3
Biographical/Historical Note	4
Scope and Content Note	6
List of Series and Subseries	10
Series Descriptions	11
Index Terms	14
Container List	15

Use of manuscript materials. If you wish to examine items in the manuscript group, please fill out a call slip specifying the materials you wish to see. Consult the Container List for location information needed on the call slip.

Photocopying. Should you wish to request photocopies, please consult a staff member before segregating items to be copied. The existing order and arrangement of unbound materials must be maintained.

Publication. Readers assume full responsibility for compliance with laws regarding copyright, literary property rights, and libel.

Permission to examine archival and manuscript materials does not constitute permission to publish. Any publication of such materials beyond the limits of fair use requires specific prior written permission. Requests for permission to publish should be addressed in writing to the Head, LLMVC, Special Collections, LSU Libraries, Baton Rouge, LA, 70803-3300. When permission to publish is granted, two copies of the publication will be requested for the LLMVC.

Proper acknowledgement of LLMVC materials must be made in any resulting writing or publications. The correct form of citation for this manuscript group is given on the summary page. Copies of scholarly publications based on research in the Louisiana and Lower Mississippi Valley Collections are welcomed.

MARSHALL-FURMAN FAMILY PAPERS   Mss 4042, 2740
1794-1975

Summary

Size.   10 linear feet (3,046 items, 35 volumes, 8 reels microfilm)

**Geographic
locations.**   Louisiana; South Carolina; Mississippi; Alabama; Arkansas;
                      Georgia; Florida; Washington, D.C.; Tennessee.

**Inclusive
dates.**   1794-1975.

**Bulk.
dates.**   1833-1905.

Summary.   Personal and business correspondence, legal, financial, and professional
                      papers, personal and political writings, maps, photographs, scrapbook
                      materials and printed items of the families and descendants of Henry
                      Marshall and S. C. Furman. Marshall was a Northwest Louisiana
                      pioneer in the 1830s and early 1840s, a planter, a member of the
                      Louisiana Secession Convention, and framer of the Confederate
                      Constitution. S. C. Furman was a doctor and military figure who
                      served in the "Pelican Rifles" of DeSoto Parish and lead a cavalry unit
                      called "Furman's Rangers."

**Related col-
lections.**   Marshall (John J.) Plantation Ledgers, Microfilm (Acc. #3025).

Source.   Gift, 1991.

Access.   No restrictions.

Copyright.   Physical rights are retained by the LSU Libraries. Copyright of the
                      original materials is retained by descendants of the creators of the
                      materials in accordance with U.S. copyright law.

Citation.   Marshall-Furman Family Papers, Louisiana and Lower Mississippi
                      Valley Collections, LSU Libraries, Baton Rouge, Louisiana.

Stack locations. W:59-68, H:1, OS:M

MARSHALL-FURMAN FAMILY PAPERS   Mss 4042, 2740
1794-1975

List of Series and Subseries

I.   Correspondence, 1807-1975
          I.1 Letters, 1811-1975 (Folders 1-160)
          I.2 Invitations, postcards, greeting cards, 1807-1975 (Folders 161-185)

II.   Financial papers, 1794-1975 (Folders 199-220)

III.   Legal documents, 1829-1937 (Folders 221-226)

IV.   Professional records, 1850-1943 (Folders 227-232)

V.   Political materials, 1833-1939 (Folders 233-237)

VI.   Personal papers, 1824-1949 (Folders 238-244)

VII.   Manuscript volumes, 1824-1865 (16 volumes)

VIII. Printed matter, 1831-1926 (Folders 245-247, 11 volumes)

IX.   Scrapbook materials, 1890-1954 (8 volumes, folders 248-251, oversized folder 257)

X.   Photographs, n.d. (Folders 252-255)

XI.   Maps, n.d. (Oversized folder 256)

XII.   Transcripts and exhibit labels, 1811-1870 (Folders 186-198)

XIII. Microfilm, 1824-1903 (8 reels)

MARSHALL-FURMAN FAMILY PAPERS   Mss 4042, 2740
1794-1975

Series Descriptions

Series I.   Correspondence, 1807-1975 (2,001 items)
   Subseries 1: Letters, 1811-1975 (1,367 items)
      Mostly letters written to and from members of the Marshall, Furman,
      and Chandler families. Topics covered include personal financial
      concerns, plantation management, military and political matters,
      education, and religion.

   Subseries 2: Invitations, postcards, greeting cards, 1807-1975 (634 items)
      Invitations to parties, weddings, graduations, and events along with
      regrets received, as well as announcements of births and letters of
      condolence. Personal postcards and seasonal greeting cards from
      family members and friends are included along with some blank
      postcards.

Series II. Financial papers, 1794-1975 (203 items)
   Includes receipts of sales of slaves and property of Adam Marshall; accounts,
   shipping invoices, and bills of sale of cotton and other agricultural products by
   Henry Marshall; bills, sales slips, a mortgage, and receipts of members of the
   Marshall and Furman families.

Series III. Legal documents, 1829-1937 (46 items)
   Labor contracts, rental contracts, military land warrants, and papers
   documenting property ownership, licenses, testamentary documents, an
   adoption paper, a birth certificate, and notes of legal procedures are included.

Series IV. Professional records, 1850-1943 (57 items)
   Documents relating to the law practices of Greene Callier Chandler and G.
   Chandler Furman, and the medical practices of S. C. Furman and F. S.
   Furman. Includes items relating to memberships in professional organizations.

Series V. Political materials, 1833-1939 (21 items)
   Addresses, papers, and speeches written by Henry Marshall, Greene C.
   Chandler, G. Chandler Furman, and Mary T. Furman. Includes election
   returns, voter registration forms, a loyalty oath, printed material related to
   political activities of family members.

Appendix D
Appraisal Checklist

1. Do the papers or records fall within the scope of the local history collection's collection development policy?

2. Do the records show the development, organizational structure, and policies of the organization for an extended period of time? Do the papers show the lifetime interests and activities of a particular individual or family?

3. Do the papers or records document legal events and activities of the person or organization?

4. Is financial documentation of the organization, person, or family included in records or papers?

5. Is the information contained in the documents duplicated in another series of records or papers or in another format within the records or papers?

6. If the papers or records are organized by the creator with a file code, file plan, register, log book, or index, are these "control records" also available?

7. Are the records "case files"? Student records, Internal Revenue Service records, medical records, veteran's records, social security application files. Those records which contain information protected by the Federal Privacy Act?

8. Do the papers or records have a distinct order or arrangement?

9. Are the records or papers complete, including enough documentation that gaps do not make them useless for research? Will there be subsequent donations?

10. What is the size of the collection? Quality versus quantity.

11. Do the papers or records contain information that must be restricted for individual privacy, government, or business security?

12. Are restrictions required by the donor? Are the papers a gift or a loan that will become a gift at a later time? [NOTE: Records of functioning organizations are only deposited in the local history collection and remain the property of the organization until it ceases to function.]

13. Do the restrictions have an established time limitation?

14. What is the physical form of the papers or records?

15. What is the physical condition of the papers or records?

16. What is the significance of the creator of the papers or records?

17. Has any of the material been published?

18. Is any known significant research being done in the field represented by the papers or records?

19. Does the local history collection have related collections and materials?

20. Are the papers or records being split among repositories? Are portions of them already in another repository?

21. What are the time periods covered?

22. Will copyright and other literary rights be transferred to the local history collection with the papers, or at a later time?[1]

23. For organizational and governmental records, the following appraisal questions are necessary:

    a. Which units of the organization have responsibility for policies, procedures, programs, and decision making?
    b. What records are vital records? A vital record is "a record containing information essential to reestablish or continue an organization in the event of a disaster. Vital records comprise the records necessary to recreate the organization's legal and financial status, and to determine the rights and obligations of employees, customers, stockholders, and citizens."[2]
    c. What activity or area of responsibility of the agency or agency function do the records reflect?
    d. What records show how all functions of the organization are carried out?
    e. Is the information contained unique and/or the records containing the information unique?[3]

The appraisal checklist can be compiled as a questionnaire for yes/no or short answers, or the checklist questions can be weighted. For example, question 1, "Do the papers or records fall within the local history collection's policy?":

No   1   2   3   4   Yes

This can be applied when a collection of papers or records hold some items that fall within the local history collection's collection development policy and other items that do not. The weight given to the questions can be decided by the percentage of materials which would not be within the collection development policy and those that would: 10% might equal "1",

20% = "2", and so on. A guideline can be developed to accept materials that receive more than a certain number of points on the appraisal checklist and to reject those that do not receive the required number of points. The appraisal checklist can also be formulated into "decision tables" or flow charts.[4]

Notes

1. Barbara Reed, "Acquisition and Appraisal," in *Keeping Archives*, Ann Pederson, ed. (Sydney, Australia: Australian Society of Archivists, 1987), 96-100, 110-113.

2. Lewis J. Bellardo and Lynn Lady Bellardo, comps., *A Glossary for Archivists, Manuscript Curators, and Records Managers* (Chicago: Society of American Archivists, 1992), 37.

3. T. R. Schellenberg, "The Appraisal of Modern Public Records," in *A Modern Archives Reader*, Maygene Daniels and Timothy Walch, eds. (Washington, DC: National Archives Trust Fund Board, 1984), 61, 63-67.

4. See for example, Figure 1, Archival Considerations, in Charles M. Dollar, "Appraising Machine-Readable Records," in *A Modern Archives Reader*, Daniels and Walch, eds., 75.

Bibliography

"American Memory from the Library of Congress: A Catalog of Collections in Preparation and Under Consideration." Washington, DC: Library of Congress, 1991.

Anglo-American Cataloguing Rules, Second Edition, 1988 Revision. Chicago: American Library Association, 1986.

Banks, Paul N. *A Selective Bibliography on the Conservation of Research Library Materials.* Chicago: Newberry Library, 1981.

Baum, Willa K. *Transcribing and Editing Oral History.* Nashville, TN: American Association for State and Local History, 1977.

Bellardo, Lewis J., and Lynn Lady Bellardo, comps. *A Glossary for Archivists, Manuscript Curators, and Records Managers.* Chicago: Society of American Archivists, 1992.

Billington, James H. "Library of Congress to Open Collections to Local Libraries in Electronic Access Plans." *American Libraries* 22 (1991): 706-709.

Bonk, Wallace John, and Rose Mary Magrill. *Building Library Collections.* 5th ed. Metuchen, NJ: Scarecrow Press, 1979.

BookLab. *BookNote 2: Salvage of Library Materials from Water or Insect Damage.* Austin, TX: BookLab, not dated.

———. *BookNote 4: Safe Handling and Exhibition of Books.* Austin, TX: BookLab, not dated.

Cave, Roderick. *Rare Book Librarianship.* London: Clive Bingley, 1976.

Christensen, John O., et al. "An Evaluation of Reference Desk Service." *College and Research Libraries* 50 (1989): 468-483.

Conrad, James H. *Developing Local History Programs in Community Libraries.* Chicago: American Library Association, 1989.

Crews, Kenneth D. "Unpublished Manuscripts and the Right of Fair Use: Copyright Law and the Strategic Management of Information Resources." *Rare Books and Manuscripts Librarianship* 5 (1990): 61-70.

Cunha, George. "Current Trends in Preservation Research and Development." *American Archivist* 53 (1990): 192-202.

Cunha, George, and Dorothy Cunha. *Library and Archives Conservation: 1980s and Beyond.* 2 vols. Metuchen, NJ: Scarecrow Press, 1983.

Curtin, Bonnie Rose. "Preservation Planning for Archives: Development and Field Testing of the NAGARA GRASP." *American Archivist* 53 (1990): 236-248.

Daniels, Maygene F., and Timothy Walch, eds. *A Modern Archives Reader: Basic Readings on Archival Theory and Practice.* Washington, DC: National Archives Trust Fund Board, 1984.

Dewe, Michael, ed. *A Manual of Local Studies Librarianship.* Aldershot, England: Gower, 1987.

———. *Local Studies Collections: A Manual.* Vol. 2 Aldershot, England: Gower, 1991.

Directory of Consultants. Chicago: Society of American Archivists, 1992.

Directory of Genealogical Software: Your Guide to the Genealogy Software Market Today. Salt Lake City, UT: Ancestry, 1990.

Directory of Historical Agencies in North America. 14th ed. Nashville, TN: American Association for State and Local History, 1990.

Directory to Fulltext Online Resources 1992. Westport, CT: Meckler, 1992.

Dolnick, Sandy, ed. *Friends of Libraries Source Book.* Chicago: American Library Association, 1990.

Drucker, Peter F. *The Effective Executive.* New York: Harper & Row, 1967.

Duckett, Kenneth. *Modern Manuscripts.* Nashville, TN: American Association for State and Local History, 1976.

Espy, Siri N. *Handbook of Strategic Planning for Nonprofit Organizations.* New York: Praeger Publishers, 1986.

Ferguson, Anthony W., Joan Grant, and Joel S. Rutstein. The RLG Conspectus: Its Uses and Benefits." *College and Research Libraries* 49 (1988): 197-206.

Firsching, Donald. "Information Sharing Through Standardization: Minaret at the National Archives of the Episcopal Church." *The Southwestern Archivist* 16 (1991): 6-8, 32-34.

Flanders, Bruce L. "Barbarians at the Gate." *American Libraries* 22 (1991): 668-669.

Ford, Sylverna. "The Library Newsletter, Is It for You?" *College and Research Libraries News* 49 (1988): 678-682.

Friends of Libraries, U.S.A. *The Best Ideas 1979-1989*. Bridgewater, NJ: Baker and Taylor, 1989.

Garlick, Karen. "Planning an Effective Holdings Maintenance Program." *American Archivist* 53 (1990): 256-264.

Gertz, Janet E. "Preservation Microfilming for Archives and Manuscripts." *American Archivist* 53 (1990): 223-234.

Gracy, II, David B. *Archives and Manuscripts: Arrangement and Description*. Chicago: Society of American Archivists, 1977.

Gross, Alfred, and Walter Gross, eds. *Business Policy*. New York: Ronald Press, 1967.

Gwinn, Nancy E., ed. *Preservation Microfilming: A Guide for Librarians and Archivists*. Chicago: American Library Association, 1987.

Hackman, Larry J., and Joan Warnow-Blewett. "The Documentation Strategy Process: A Model and a Case Study." *American Archivist* 50 (1987): 12-47.

Haeuser, Michael; and Evelyn Riche Olivier. "Effective Public Relations Programs Benefit Academic Libraries." *College and Research Libraries News* 50 (1989): 490-493.

Henson, Steven. *Archives, Personal Papers, and Manuscripts*. 2d ed. Chicago: Society of American Archivists, 1989.

Jenkins, Barbara Williams, and Mary L. Smalls. *Performance Appraisal in Academic Libraries*. CLIP Note #12. Chicago: Association of College and Research Libraries, 1990.

Katz, William A. *Introduction to Reference Services*. 6th ed. 2 vols. New York: McGraw-Hill, 1992.

Landis, Lawrence A. "Cataloguing Software and the University Archives: MicroMARC: AMC at the Oregon State University. *The Southwestern Archivist* 16 (1991): 6-8, 32.

Lawrence, Priscilla O' Reilly. *Before Disaster Strikes: Prevention, Planning and Recovery*. New Orleans: The Historic New Orleans Collection, 1992.

LC Information Bulletin. Washington, DC: Library of Congress.

Lynn, M. Stuart. *Preservation and Access Technology, the Relationship Between Digital and Other Media Conversion Processes: A Structured Glossary of Technical Terms*. Washington, DC: The Commission on Preservation and Access, 1990.

Makepeace, Chris E. *Ephemera: A Book on Its Collection, Conservation and Use.* Aldershot, England: Gower, 1985.

Miller, Fredric M. *Arranging and Describing Archives and Manuscripts.* Chicago: Society of American Archivists, 1990.

Moss, William W. *Oral History Program Manual.* New York: Greenwood Press, 1986.

National Association of Government Archives and Records Administrators. *Guide and Resources for Archives Strategic Preservation Planning.* Lexington, KY: Council of State Governments, 1992.

Oberg, Larry R. "Evaluating the Conspectus Approach for Small Library Collections." *College and Research Libraries* 49 (1988): 187-196.

Parker, J. Carlyle. *Library Service for Genealogists.* Gale Genealogy and Local History Series, vol. 15. Detroit, MI: Gale Research, 1981.

Peace, Nancy, ed. *Archival Choices: Managing the Historical Record in an Age of Abundance.* Lexington, MA: Lexington Books, 1984.

Pederson, Ann E., ed. *Keeping Archives.* Sydney, Australia: Australian Society of Archivists, 1987.

Pederson, Ann E., and Gail Farr Casterline. *Archives and Manuscripts: Public Programs.* Chicago: Society of American Archivists, 1982.

Penn, Ira A., Anne Morddel, Gail Dennis, and Kevin Smith. *Records Management Handbook.* New York: Gower, 1989.

Peterson, Gary, and Trudy H. Peterson. *Archives and the Law.* Chicago: Society of American Archivists, 1985.

Peterson, Trudy H. "The Gift and the Deed." *American Archivist* 42 (1979): 61-66.

Phillips, Faye. "Developing Collecting Policies for Manuscript Collections." *American Archivist* 47 (1984): 30-42.

Public Interest Public Relations. *Promoting Issues and Ideas: A Guide to Public Relations for Nonprofit Organizations.* New York: The Foundation Center, 1987.

Pugh, Mary Jo. *Providing Reference Services for Archives and Manuscripts.* Chicago: Society of American Archivists, 1992.

Reed, Henry Hope. *The New York Public Library: Its Architecture and Decoration.* New York: W. W. Norton, 1986.

Ritzenthaler, Mary Lynn *Archives and Manuscripts: Conservation.* Chicago: Society of American Archivists, 1983.

Ritzenthaler, Mary Lynn, Gerald Munoff, and Margery S. Long. *Archives and Manuscripts: Administration of Photographic Collections.* Chicago: Society of American Archivists, 1984.

Russo, David J. *Families and Communities: A New View of American History.* Nashville, TN: American Association for State and Local History, 1974.

Samules, Helen. "Who Controls the Past?" *American Archivist* 49 (1986): 109-124.

Sanford, Al. *Computer Genealogy Notebook* 1. Garland, TX: Al Sanford Publisher, 1992.

Schreiner-Yantis, Netti, comp. *Genealogical and Local History Books in Print.* 4th ed. and supplements. Springfield, VA: Genealogical Books in Print, 1990.

Sinko, Peggy Tuck. *Guide to Local and Family History at the Newberry Library.* Salt Lake City, UT: Ancestry Publishing, 1987.

Smith, Karen F. "Robot at the Reference Desk?" *College and Research Libraries* 47 (1986): 486-490.

Smith, Page. *As a City upon a Hill: The Town in American History.* New York: Alfred A. Knopf, 1966.

Stearns, Peter N., ed. *Expending the Past: A Reader in Social History, Essays from the Journal of Social History.* New York: New York University Press, 1988.

Stueart, Robert D., and John Taylor Eastlick. *Library Management.* 2d ed. Littleton, CO: Libraries Unlimited, 1981

Stueart, Robert D., and George B. Miller, Jr. *Collection Development in Libraries: A Treatise.* Greenwich, CT: JAI Press, 1980.

Stueart, Robert D., and Barbara B. Moran. *Library Management.* 3d ed. Englewood, CO: Libraries Unlimited, 1987.

Thompson, Enid T. *Local History Collections: A Manual for Librarians.* Nashville, TN: American Association for State and Local History, 1978.

Trinkaus-Randall, Gregor. "Preserving Special Collections Through Internal Security." *College and Research Libraries* 50 (1989): 448-454.

Walch, Timothy. *Archives and Manuscripts: Security.* Chicago: Society of American Archivists, 1977.

Waters, Peter. *Emergency Procedures for Salvaging Flood or Water Damaged Library Materials.* 2d ed. Washington, DC: Library of Congress, 1979.

Weinstein, Robert A., and Larry Booth. *Collection, Use, and Care of Historical Photographs.* Nashville, TN: American Association for State and Local History, 1977.

Wilsted, Thomas, and William Nolte. *Managing Archival and Manuscript Repositories.* Chicago: Society of American Archivists, 1991.

Wyly, Mary P. "Special Collections Security: Problems, Trends, and Consciousness." *Library Trends* 36 (1987): 241-255.

Zaltman, Gerald, ed. *Management Principles for Nonprofit Agencies and Organizations.* New York: American Management Association, 1979.

Zinkham, Helena, Patricia D. Cloud, and Hope Mayo. "Providing Access by Form of Materials, Genre, and Physical Characteristics: Benefits and Techniques." *American Archivist* 52 (1989): 300-319.

Index

AB Bookman's Weekly, 19
Access, 37-51
"Access and Reference Services"
    (Hinchey and McCausland), 35
Accession records, 42-43(fig.)
Accessioning, 41
Acquisitions, 19-28, 134
    agreement form, 23-25(fig.)
"Acquisition and Appraisal" (Reed), 149
Administration, 119-32
ALA. *See* American Library Association
American Antiquarian Society, 113
American Association for State and
        Local History, 1, 9
    address, 34
    exhibitions, 106
    historical photographs, 6
    oral history publications, 114
    professional involvement, 124
    program ideas, 117
American Association of Museums, 106
American Library Association
    address, 34
    Books for College Libraries, 16
    collection development policy, 10
    guidelines for friends organiza-
        tions, 111
    professional involvement, 124
    program ideas, 117
American Memory Project, 74-75, 78
American National Standards Institute
        (ANSI), 65-66
    standards, 65-66
*Anglo-American Cataloguing Rules,
    Second Edition,* 38-40, 50
ANSI. *See* American National Standards
    Institute
"The Appraisal of Modern Public
        Records" (Schellenberg), 98, 149
Appraisals
    archival, 29-32
    checklist, 147-49
    criteria, 28-29
    definition, 28
    manuscripts, 20, 32-33
    tax, 26-27
"Appraising Machine-Readable Records"
        (Dollar), 149

*Archival Choices: Managing the His-
    torical Record in an Age of
    Abundance* (Peace), 35
Archival Fundamental Series (Society
    for American Archivists), 1, 9
*Archival Storage Materials and Con-
    servation Supplies Catalogue,*
    72
Archives
    accessioning, 41-44(fig.)
    appraisal, 29-32(fig.)
    arrangement and description, 41-
        50(fig.)
    definition, 4-5
    restrictions of use, 27
*Archives and Manuscripts: Administra-
    tion of Photographic Collections*
    (Ritzenthaler, Munoff, and
    Long), 9, 71
*Archives and Manuscripts: Arrangement
    and Description* (Gracy), 51
*Archives and Manuscripts: Conserva-
    tion* (Ritzenthaler), 70(fig.),
    71
*Archives and Manuscripts: Public
    Programs* (Pederson and
    Casterline), 102, 117
Archives and Manuscripts: Security
    (Walch), 71
Archives and the Law (Peterson and
    Peterson), 35, 98
*Archives, Personal Papers and Manu-
    scripts II (APPMII)* (Hensen),
    47, 49
Archivists, qualifications, 121
*Arranging and Describing Archives
    and Manuscripts* (Miller), 46, 51
Art and Architecture Thesaurus, 51
Artifacts, 6-7
*As a City upon a Hill: The Town in
    American History* (Smith), 9
Association of Research Libraries, 16,
    82
Association of Shareware Professionals,
    78
Atlanta Historical Society, 55(fig.),
    61(fig.), 93-94(fig.)
Audiovisual materials, 4, 5-7

"Barbarians at the Gate" (Flanders), 51
Basic Manual Series (Society of
        American Archivists), 1, 9
Baum, Willa K., 118
*Before Disaster Strikes: Prevention,
        Planning, and Recovery*
        (Lawrence), 72
Bellardo, Lewis J., 9, 72, 117, 149
Bellardo, Lynn Lady, 9, 72, 117, 149
Bibliographical
    database networks, 38-39. *See also*
        OCLC, RLIN, WLN
    records, 48(fig.)
Bibliographies, 50, 88
Billington, James H., 74, 78
Bonk, Wallach John, 34
*BookNote 2: Salvage of Library Mate-
        rials from Water or Insect
        Damage*, 72
*BookNote 4: Safe Handling and
        Exhibition of Books*, 117
Books for College Libraries, 16
Books in Print Plus, 91
Booth, Larry, 9
Brittle Books project, 79
Brochures, 52, 90, 91, 103
Budget definitions, 128 (fig.)
Budgeting, 126-32
Buffalo Bill Cody Museum, 8
Building Library Collections (Bonk
        and Magrill), 34
Business Policy (Gross and Gross), 132

Call slips, 53-55(fig.)
Card catalogs, 37, 49
Casterline, Gail Farr, 100, 102, 117
Cataloging, 1, 7, 38-41
"Cataloguing Software and the Univer-
        sity Archives: MicroMARC:
        AMC at Oregon State
        University" (Landis), 51
Cave, Roderick, 27
Chadwyck-Healey, Inc., 49, 51
Chalou, George, 98
Christensen, John O., 98
Church of Jesus Christ of Latter-Day
        Saints, 66
Circulation, 52-53
Classification, 16, 38-39
Clientele. *See* Patrons
Cloud, Patricia D., 51
Collection
    classification, 16

development policies, 10-12, 133-36
    evaluation, 16
*Collection Development in Libraries:
        A Treatise* (Stueart and
        Miller), 11, 35
*Collection, Use, and Care of Historical
        Photographs* (Weinstein and
        Booth), 9
Commercial software and hardware,
        75-78
Commission on Preservation and
        Access, 79
Community programs. *See* Outreach
        programs
Computer Genealogy Notebook, 78
Computer
    catalogs, 37-39, 44, 49
    generated historical materials, 6,
        74-75
    networks, 77-78
    searches, 91
Congressional Research Center, 113
Conservation, 52-71(fig.)
Cooke, Robert A., 35
Cooperative agreements, 14-15, 16,
        135
Copyright, 21-26(fig.), 86-88(fig.), 92,
        120, 132
Cornell University, 77
Council on Library Resources, Inc., 34
Cunha, George, 71, 72
Cunha, Dorothy, 71, 72
Curtin, Bonnie Rose, 72

Daniels, Maygene, 9, 35, 36, 51, 98,
        132, 149
Deaccessioning, 15, 136
"Deaccessioning Collections: A New
        Perspective on a Continuing
        Controversy" (Dowler), 35
Deeds, 21, 23-24(fig.)
Desiderata, 19
Desktop publishing, 103
"Developing Collecting Policies for
        Manuscript Collections"
        (Phillips), 34
Dewe, Michael, 78
Dewey Decimal classification, 16,
        38-39
DIALOG, 91
Dictionary of American Biography, 3
Directory of Consultants, 72

Directory of Genealogical Software: Your Guide to the Genealogy Software Market Today, 78
Directory of Historical Agencies in North America, 98
Directory to Fulltext Online Resources 1992, 79
Disaster planning, 71
Documentation strategies, 17-19(fig.), 137-40
"The Documentation Strategy Process: A Model and a Case Study" (Hackman and Warnow-Blewett), 35
Dollar, Charles, M., 149
Dolnick, Sandy, 117
Donors, 21-28
Dowler, Lawrence, 35
Drawings, measured, 5
Drucker, Peter, 122-23, 125, 132
Duckett, Kenneth, 11, 35

Eastlick, John Taylor, 35
The Effective Executive (Drucker), 132
"Effective Public Relations Programs Benefit Academic Libraries" (Haeuser and Olivier), 118
Electronic mail, 77
Emergency Procedures for Salvaging Flood or Water Damaged Library Materials (Waters), 72
Employees. *See also* Volunteer programs
  grant-funded, 123-24
  performance evaluations, 122-24
  staffing, 121-22
  student, 123
Endowments, 131-32
Environmental controls, 53, 63-64, 107
Environmental Protection Agency, 56
ERIC, 91
Espy, Siri N., 132
Evaluating
  collections, 16, 134
  programs, 108-10(fig.), 115-17
  staff performance, 122-24
"Evaluating the Conspectus Approach for Small Library Collections" (Oberg), 35
"An Evaluation of Reference Desk Services" (Christensen), 98
Exhibitions, 106-10(fig.), 133-34
Exhibits, 12-13

Expanding the Past: A Reader in Social History, Essays from the Journal of Social History (Stearns), 9

Fair use of copyrighted materials, 26, 86-87(fig.), 92
Families and Communities: A New View of American History (Russo), 2, 9
Family papers, 4, 33, 141-46(fig.)
Fax transmission of historical data, 77
Federal Copyright Act. *See* U.S. Code, Title 17
Federal grant agencies, 129(fig.)
Federal Privacy Act, 27
Fellowships, 113
Fiber optics, 73
Films, 6
Finding aids, 47-49, 66. *See also* Research guides
Fire prevention, 53-56
Firsching, Donald, 51
Flanders, Bruce L., 51
Ford, Sylverna, 117
Formats of historical materials, 5-7
Foundation Center, 130
Foundation Directory, 130
French, B. F., 75
Friends of Libraries Source Book (Dolnick), 117
Friends organizations, 20, 110-11

Genealogical and Local History Books in Print (Schreiner-Yantis), 77-78
Genealogical reference file, 91
Genealogical Society of Utah, 72
"The Gift and the Deed" (Peterson), 35, 36
Gifts
  acquisitions, 21-28(fig.)
  forms, 23-25(fig.)
  restrictions of use, 85-86
A Glossary for Archivists, Manuscript Curators, and Records Managers (Bellardo and Bellardo), 9, 72, 117, 149
Government documents, 5, 40, 88
Gracy, David B., 51
Grant-funded employees, 123-24
Grants, 129-31(fig.)
Gross, Alfred, 132

Gross, Walter, 132
Guide and Resources for Archives Strategic Preservation Planning (GRASP) (NAGARA), 72
Guide to Local and Family History at the Newberry Library (Sinko), 9
"Guidelines for the Formulation of Collection Development Policies" (ALA), 34
"Guidelines for the Security of Rare Book Manuscripts and Other Special Collections," 82, 98
Gwinn, Nancy E., 72

Hackman, Larry J., 35
Haeuser, Michael, 118
Handbook of Strategic Planning for Nonprofit Organizations (Espy), 132
Handling of historic materials, 57
Henry E. Huntington Library and Art Gallery, 80
Hensen, Steve, 47
Higginson, M. Valliant, 132
Higher Education Act, 129
Hinchey, Sandra, 35
Historical Collections of Louisiana, Embracing Many Rare and Valuable Documents Related to the Natural, Civil and Political History of that State (French), 75, 79
Historical societies, 8, 80
Hubbard, L. Ron, 88
Huntington Library, 8

Imaging software, 76-77
Identification, patron, 13, 81-82
Indexes, 50, 76
"Information Sharing Through Standardization: Minaret at the National Archives of the Episcopal Church" (Firsching), 51
"Information Technology" (Seton), 78
Insect damage, 63-64
Institute of Museum Services, 129
Internal Revenue Service, 26
"Introduction to Archival Terminology" (Daniels), 36, 51
Introduction to Reference Services (Katz), 84, 98

Inventories, 47-49, 141-46
IRS. *See* Internal Revenue Service

Jenkins, Barbara Williams, 132
Job descriptions, 121-22
Journals, 105-106
"Justices Permit Strict Curbs on Use of Unpublished Writings," 98

Katz, William A., 84, 98
Keeping Archives (Pederson), 35, 149

Landis, Lawrence A., 51
Lawrence, Priscilla O'Reilly, 72
LDS Church, 66
Lectures, 110
Librarians, qualifications, 121
Libraries
   public, 7-8, 10, 80
   special, 8, 10, 80
   university, 7, 10, 80
Library and Archives Conservation: 1980's and Beyond (Cunha and Cunha), 71-72
Library and Information Resources for the Northwest, 16
Library Management (Stueart and Eastlick), 35
Library Management, 3d ed. (Stueart and Moran), 128, 132
"The Library Newsletter, Is It for You?" (Ford), 117
Library of Congress
   American Memory Project, 74-75, 78
   cataloging, 38-39
   classification, 16, 38
   copyright office, 26, 87
   National Register of Microform Masters, 66
   National Union Catalog of Manuscript Collections, 15
   Register of Copyrights, 86
Library of Congress Information Bulletin, 79
Library of Congress Name Authorities, 40
Library of Congress Subject Headings, 40-41, 49
"Library of Congress to Open Collections to Local Libraries in Electronic Access Plans" (Billington), 78

Lighting, 63, 107
Local history
  audiovisual materials, 4
  definition, 2
  formats, 5-7
  manuals, 1, 9
  professional associations, 33-34
  reference books, 3-4
  statement of purpose, 12-13
  types, 3-5(fig.), 37
*Local History Collections: A Manual
    for Librarians* (Thompson), 1,
    9, 35
*Local Studies Collections: A Manual,
    Volume 2* (Dewe), 78
Long, Margery S., 9, 71
Long-range planning, 125-26
Louisiana and Lower Mississippi
    Valley Collections, 7, 79
  accession record, 43(fig.)
  call slip, 54(fig.)
  collection development policy state-
    ment, 133-36
  Electronic Imaging Laboratory, 75
  insect control, 63-64
  inventory, 141-46
  manuscript removal form, 97(fig.)
  preservation log, 69(fig.)
  processing report, 68(fig.)
  program visitor questionnaire,
    109(fig.)
  reference letters, 91
  regulations for readers, 62(fig.)
  staffing, 121
  subject bibliographies, 88-90(fig.)
  volunteer form, 112(fig.)
Louisiana Endowment for the
    Humanities, 130
Louisiana State University, 7, 79, 116
  Friends of the Library, 110
Lynn, M. Stuart, 78

Machine readable cataloging, 47
Machine readable historical records, 6
Magrill, Rose Mary, 34
Mailing lists, 104-105
Maiman, Theodor, 73
Management, 119-32
Management (Drucker), 132
"Management Concepts and Archival
    Administration" (Worthy), 132
*Management of Oral History Sound
    Archives* (Stielow), 118

*Managing Archival and Manuscript
    Repositories* (Wilsted and
    Nolte), 132
"Managing Change in Organizations"
    (Cooke), 35
*Managing Principles for Nonprofit
    Agencies and Organizations*
    (Zaltman), 35
Manuals, procedure, 120-21
Manuscripts
  accessioning, 41-44(fig.)
  appraisals, 20, 32-33
  arrangement and description, 41-
    50(fig.)
  definition, 4-5
  purchasing, 19-21
  removal form, 97(fig.)
  restrictions of use, 27
  tax appraisals, 26
Maps, 5
MARC format, 47
Marshall-Furman Family Papers, 141-
    46(fig.)
Mayo, Hope, 51
McCausland, Sigrid, 35
Measured drawings, 5
Media outreach programs, 114
Microfilming, 64-66, 86, 92
Microform Masters, 66
Microforms, 5
  readers, 96
MicroMARC-AMC, 44
Midwest Archives Conference, 33
Miller, George B., 11, 35
Miller, Frederic M., 46, 51
Minaret, 44
Mission statements, 12-13
*A Modern Archives Reader: Basic
    Reading on Archival Theory and
    Practice* (Daniels and Walch),
    9, 35, 36, 51, 98, 132, 149
Modern Manuscripts (Duckett), 35
Moran, Barbara B., 128, 132
Moss, William W., 118
Munoff, Gerald, 9, 71
Museums, 8, 81

National Archives, 28, 47
National Archives and Records
    Administration, 56
National Association of Government
    Archives and Records Adminis-
    trators (NAGARA), 72

National Endowment for the Arts, 129
National Endowment for the Humanities, 13, 114, 126, 128-29, 131
National Historical Publications and Records Commission, 34, 129, 131
National Register of Microform Masters, 66
National Science Foundation, 129
National Union Catalog, 39
National Union Catalog of Manuscript Collections, 15, 50, 66, 77, 90
NEA. *See* National Endowment for the Arts
NEH. *See* National Endowment for the Humanities
New York Public Library, 7
The New York Public Library: Its Architecture and Decoration (Reed), 9
Newberry Library, 8, 113
Newsletters, 103-105
NHPRC. *See* National Historical Publications and Records Commission
Nolte, William, 132
Nonprint materials. *See* Audiovisual materials
North American Collections Inventory Project, 16
NOTIS, 39, 48, 50
NSF. *See* National Science Foundation
NUC. *See* National Union Catalog

Oberg, Larry R., 35
OCLC, 1, 15, 38-39, 47-48, 50, 77, 91
  United States Newspaper Project, 131
The Official Records of the War of the Rebellion, 4
Olivier, Evelyn Riche, 118
Online Computer Library Center. *See* OCLC
Online computer searches, 91
Optical scanners, 75-76
Oral history, 6, 114-15
  release form, 116(fig.)
Oral History Association, 114
Oral History Program Manual (Moss), 118
Organizational records. *See* Archives
Organizations, 33-34
Original
  cataloging, 1, 38, 40

order of records, 31, 32
Outreach
  programs, 13, 99-100, 106-17(fig.), 134
  projects, 113-15

Pamphlets, 5, 40
Patrons, 80-97, 134
  identification, 13, 81-82
  request forms, 58-62(fig.)
Peace, Nancy, 35
Pederson, Ann E., 35, 100, 102, 117, 149
Performance Appraisal in Academic Libraries (Jenkins and Smalls), 132
Performance evaluations, 122-24
Personnel, 84, 121-22
Peterson, Gary, 35, 98
Peterson, Trudy H., 21, 35, 36, 98
Pew Charitable Trust, 130
Phillips, Faye, 34
Photocopying, 63, 86, 96
Photoduplication request, 95(fig.)
Photographs, 5-6, 92-94(fig.)
Pierpoint Morgan Library, 8
Planning, 100, 124-26
Planning for the Archival Profession: A Report of the SAA Task Force on Goals and Priorities (Society of American Archivists), 125
Policies for administration, 119-21
Preservation, 52-71, 133
  supplies, 56(fig.), 67(fig.)
Preservation and Access Technology, the Relationship Between Digital and Other Media Conversion Processes: A Structured Glossary of Technical Terms (Lynn), 78
Preservation Microfilming: A Guide for Librarians and Archivists (Gwinn), 72
"Preservation Planning for Archives: Development and Field Testing of the NAGARA GRASP" (Curtin), 72
"Preserving Special Collections Through Internal Security" (Trinkaus-Randall), 98
Press releases, 101-103(fig.), 108
"A Primer on Manuscript Field Work" (Stewart), 35
Privacy Act, 88
Procedures manuals, 120-21

Processing, 66-69(fig.)
Professional associations, 33-34, 124
Program priorities, 14
Promoting Issues and Ideas: A Guide to Public Relations for Nonprofit Organizations, 118
Provenance-based arrangement, 44-45
"Providing Access by Form of Material, Genre and Physical Characteristics: Benefits and Techniques" (Zinkham, Cloud, and Mayo), 51
Providing Reference Services for Archives and Manuscripts (Pugh), 98
Public libraries, 7-8, 10, 80
Public relations, 99-106(fig.)
Publications
    programs, 13, 134
    restrictions, 88, 92
Publicity. *See* Press releases
Pugh, Mary Jo, 98
Purchasing historical materials, 19
"Putting Policies in Context" (Higginson), 132

Rare book dealers, 19-20
Rare Book Librarianship (Cave), 27
Records retention schedules, 30(fig.)
Reed, Barbara, 149
Reed, Henry Hope, 9
Reference
    books, 3-4, 85
    letters, 91
    services, 83-86
"Reference" (Chalou), 98
Regional history. *See* Local history
Request forms, 58-62(fig.)
Research, 133
    fellowships, 113
    guides, 89-90(fig.). *See also* Finding aids
Research Libraries Group, 16
Research Libraries Information Network. *See* RLIN
Resource-sharing, 14-15, 16, 136
Restrictions of use, 27, 85-86, 92
Ritzenthaler, Mary Lynn, 9, 70, 71
RLG. *See* Research Libraries Group
RLG Conspectus, 16
RLIN, 1, 15, 38-39, 44, 47-48(fig.), 50, 77, 91

"Robot at the Reference Desk?" (Smith), 98
Russo, David J., 2, 9

Salinger, J. D., 88
Samuels, Helen, 35
Sanborn Fire Insurance Company maps, 5
Scanners, 75-76
Schellenberg, T. R., 28-29, 36, 98, 149
Schreiner-Yantis, Netti, 77-78
Security measures, 52-53, 81-83, 106-107, 133
Serials, 5
Series, 31(fig.), 45-46(fig.)
Seton, Mike, 78
Shareware, 78
Shelving, 56
Sheppard's Book Dealers in North American 1986-87: A Directory of Antiquarian and Second-hand Book Dealers in the USA and Canada, 19
Short-range planning, 126
Sinko, Peggy Tuck, 9
Smalls, Mary L., 132
Smith, Page, 9
Smith, Karen F., 98
Smithsonian Institution, 106
Social history, 2
Society of American Archivists, 1, 2, 9
    access policy, 81, 98
    address, 33
    exhibition manuals, 106
    historical photographs, 6
    long-range planning, 125
    preservation, 67
    professional involvement, 124
Society of Georgia Archivists, 33
SOLINET, 1, 15
Southeastern Library Network. *See* SOLINET
"Special Collections Security: Problems, Trends, and Consciousness" (Wyly), 98
Special libraries, 8, 10, 80
Staffing, 84, 121-22
Stand-alone computer systems, 39
"Standards for Access to Research Materials in Archival and Manuscripts Repositories," 81, 98
State government documents, 40
Statement of purpose, 12-13, 133

Statistics, 16
Stearns, Peter N., 9
Stewart, Virginia R., 35
Stielow, Frederick J., 118
Storage, 56
Strategic planning, 125-26
Student employees, 123
Stueart, Robert D., 11, 35, 128, 132
Subject
    bibliographies, 50, 88
    headings, 40-41, 49
Supplies, preservation, 56(fig.), 67(fig.)

Tax
    appraisals, 26-27
    laws, 29
Tax Reform Act of 1976, 26
Thompson, Enid T., 1, 9, 35
Title IIC grants, 131
Transcribing and Editing Oral History
    (Baum), 118
Trinkaus-Randall, Gregor, 98

U.S. Code, Title 17, 26, 86, 120, 132
U.S. Office of Education, 131
United States Newspaper Project, 131
University and college libraries, 7, 10,
    80
University of Michigan, 44
University of Oklahoma
    accession record, 42(fig.)
    Congressional Record Center, 113

patron request form, 59(fig.)
Western History Collections, 75, 79
Use
    policies, 81, 88
    restrictions, 27, 85-86, 92
User education. *See* Outreach programs
Users of historical collections. *See*
    Patrons
USMARC-AMC, 47

Vertical files, 40-41
Video recordings, 6
Volunteer programs, 111-13(fig.), 115

Walch, Timothy, 9, 35, 36, 51, 71, 98,
    132, 149
"Want list" of acquisitions, 19
Warnow-Blewett, Joan, 35
Waters, Peter, 72
Weeding, 15
Weinstein, Robert A., 9
Western Library Network. *See* WLN
"Who Controls the Past" (Samuels), 35
Who's Who, 3
Wilsondisc, 91
Wilsted, Thomas, 132
WLN, 1, 15
Worthy, James C., 132
Wyly, Mary P., 98

Zaltman, Gerald, 5
Zinkham, Helena, 51